A BATCH OF STRONG PULLERS.

THE
BIGGLE HORSE BOOK

A CONCISE AND PRACTICAL TREATISE ON THE HORSE

BY JACOB BIGGLE

ADAPTED TO THE NEEDS OF FARMERS AND OTHERS
WHO HAVE A KINDLY REGARD FOR THIS
NOBLE SERVITOR OF MAN

ILLUSTRATED

"Always speak to a horse as you would to a gentleman."

Skyhorse Publishing

Skyhorse Publishing books may be purchased in bulk at special discounts for sales promotion, corporate gifts, fund-raising, or educational purposes. Special editions can also be created to specifications. For details, contact the Special Sales Department, Skyhorse Publishing, 307 West 36th Street, 11th Floor, New York, NY 10018 or info@skyhorsepublishing.com.

Skyhorse® and Skyhorse Publishing® are registered trademarks of Skyhorse Publishing, Inc.®, a Delaware corporation.

Visit our website at www.skyhorsepublishing.com.

10 9 8 7 6 5 4 3 2 1

Library of Congress Cataloging-in-Publication Data is available on file.

ISBN: 978-1-62636-145-4

Printed in China

PREFACE.

The Author has not much to say by way of Preface. A portion of the material contained herein has been contributed by practical Horsemen and Veterinarians of the highest standing in the United States. It contains much of the kindly wisdom of John Tucker and the gentle thought of Harriet Biggle as they have been displayed in the pages of the *Farm Journal*. Much space has been given to the humane Training of the Horse, to his proper Housing and Feeding, to the Care of his Feet, and to the Education of the Colt. The Author is fully conscious of the incompleteness of the work, of its imperfections and omissions ; but he has done the best he could in the space allotted, and hopes his book will be of permanent value to all into whose possession it may come.

JACOB BIGGLE.

ELMWOOD FARM.

INVOCATION.

When cold and wet, please rub me dry,
And do not beat me when I shy ;
Give twice a week a hot bran mash,
With corn and oats and salt a dash ;
Ten pounds each day of hay that's free
From dust—all you should give to me ;

Feed twice a week, instead of oats,
A pair of carrots—'twill shine my coat ;
When hot, don't give me drink or grain ;
When cold, don't stand me in the rain ;
Batten my stable warm and tight,
And see that it's kept clean and light ;
In winter, blanket close and bed me deep ;—
And you'll find I'll pay you for my keep.

CONTENTS.

AN ENGLISH PLOWING SCENE.

HISTORY.

In all authentic history of the human race, we find the horse mentioned as the servant and companion of man.

When the horse was first domesticated is not known, nor do we know of what country he is a native. Central Asia, Arabia and Central Africa each claims this honor, and we will not dispute the claims of either.

In the time of Moses, horses were used in Egypt; and later on, Solomon kept and used large numbers of them. From Job's vivid description it is evident that they were used and well bred in the countries farther east. Horses are represented in the carvings on the ruins of ancient Ninevah and in the marble friezes of the Greek Parthenon. When the Romans invaded Britain, they found the natives using horses of superior quality, and took some of them back to Rome.

It is supposed that the Spaniards brought horses to South America as early as 1535, and that soon afterwards others were shipped to Paraguay. From these importations, it is thought there resulted the countless herds that have since spread over South America, and, passing the Isthmus of Panama, wandered into Mexico and California. In like manner, European settlers carried this noble animal to Australia, where, as in America, he has multiplied to a prodigious extent. He has, indeed, been diffused by the agency of man throughout the whole inhabited globe.

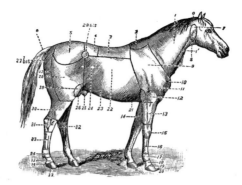

REFERENCE CHART.

0. Poll or nape of the neck.	20. Foot.
1. Neck.	21. Xiphoid region.
1′. Jugular gutter.	22. Ribs.
2. Withers.	23. Abdomen.
3. Back.	24. Flank.
4. Loins.	25. Sheath.
5. Croup.	26. Testicles.
6. Tail.	27. Buttock.
7. Parotid region.	27 *bis*. Angle of buttock.
8. Throat.	28. Thigh.
9. Shoulder.	28 *bis*. Haunch.
10. Point of the shoulder.	29. Stifle.
11. Arm.	30. Leg.
12. Elbow.	31. Hock.
13. Forearm.	32. Chestnut.
14. Chestnut.	33. Canon.
15. Knee.	34. Fetlock.
16. Canon.	35. Pastern.
17. Fetlock.	36. Coronet.
18. Pastern.	37. Foot.
19. Coronet.	

HORSE MAXIMS.

JOHN TUCKER says:

Proper food and lots of sentiment will make with good blood a good horse.

The brush will save oats.

There is a great deal of saving in a walk.

It is all right to feed the horse hay only twice a day and the most at night.

Find some way of keeping the horses busy all winter. Thus only will they keep sound and be ready for hard spring work when it comes.

It is expensive to warm ice-water inside the stock.

Horses eat dirt and gnaw their mangers from habit and because they want to.

Ask the horses if they can't help out the hay mow by eating the straw sprinkled with bran.

If you must put frosty bits in some mouths, let it be your own. Suffering begets sympathy.

HARRIET BIGGLE says:

There are oats in the currycomb.

There is more profit in coaxing than in kicks.

Do not push the plow team the first week or you may get behind.

If they throw up their heads and act timidly look after your stableman. Such acts speak louder than words.

Carry the bridles with you to the house when you go to breakfast and put the bits near the stove while you eat.

Be gentle, be kind, be patient.

Always speak to a horse as you would to a gentleman.

A horse can travel safer and better with his head hanging down or free than it can when it is checked up. By all means, let your horse have its head.

The three greatest enemies of the horse are idleness, fat and a dumb blacksmith.

Did you ever think of it? The whip is the parent of stubbornness. It is sure to be found somewhere in the pedigree of every balky horse. In training a young horse, use as intelligent brain instead of a cruel whip.

Many a horse stands up all night because its stall is not made comfortable to lie down in.

You cannot whip terror out of a horse or pound courage into one. Kindness and reasonable persuasion are the best weapons to use in training and educating a horse. If he shies or frightens, soothe and encourage him, rather than beat and abuse him.

> Give to me nutritious food;
> Give me water pure and good;
> When the chilling winds do blow,
> Over me a blanket throw;
> Shield me from all cruelty;
> When I'm old be kind to me.

CHAPTER I.

THE DIFFERENT BREEDS.

Realizing that lack of space forbids a description of every breed and type of horse, it is our aim to describe only a few breeds that fad and fancy, which often mean practical utility, have brought to the front of modern popularity.

Although the effort to improve the breeds of horses must have existed at all times, it has only been within the last few centuries that records have been preserved to us as to how this end has been sought and accomplished.

The horse whose record has been most carefully preserved, and who no doubt has left a deeper imprint on most of the modern breeds of horses, is the English Thoroughbred. Although "Thoroughbred" is apt to bring to the mind the breeding of horses for racing purposes alone, we must not forget that the qualities of courage, endurance and intelligence have largely been derived through the Thoroughbred strain, and that good blood of any kind is apt to give stronger muscles, finer bones, better joints, and superior wind and lung power.

It was during the reign of Queen Anne, in 1702–1704, that there was imported by a Mr. Darley an Arabian horse, which was called Darley's Arabian, and from him almost all of the famous horses of later day were descended. But whatever we owe to the great number of horses which were imported into England, both before and after this time, much credit is unquestionably due to the native mares, which some authorities say were mostly Cleveland Bays, upon which the Arabian, Barb or Turk was grafted, and which laid the foundation for the modern Thoroughbred. By "thorough-bred" is meant a horse or mare that can trace for generations from sires and dams of pure blood, or from Arabs, Barbs or Persians, recorded in the stud-book kept for that purpose.

Our illustration, made from a photograph from life, shows an Arabian horse, "Missirli," one of two presented to Gen-

GEN. GRANT'S ARABIAN.

eral Grant by the Sultan of Turkey about the time of the Centennial.

THE CLEVELAND BAY

constituted a well-established breed in the Cleveland district, Yorkshire, Eng., as long ago as 1740. It was named from the location and his invariable color, ranging from light to very dark bay. For at least 150 years the Cleveland Bay has been renowned as deep enough in breeding to insure transmission of his popular and solid constitution and bay color, and has been considered the best general-purpose horse bred in England. During that time a few farmers kept the blood of the Cleveland Bay pure, and refused to mix it with other horses of the district. Some of the long-time farm leases of Yorkshire provide that the favorite Cleveland Bay mare and her progeny should be bred pure

CLEVELAND BAY FILLY.

on that farm during the term of the lease, and this has preserved the breed in all its renowned essentials. Thirty years ago a few breeders thus owned most of the mares that had been bred pure, when a sudden demand sprung up for horses with level heads, good constitution, large bone and endurance, and drew attention to this breed. Then its friends were rewarded by large prices for their horses. From that time they have been most carefully bred. They are especially desirable for family teams because of their fine style and action, level heads and good disposition. They are intelligent, sensible, good roadsters, and stylish. For this reason they are unexcelled as teams for wealthy city men who are willing and able to pay a good price.

THE YORKSHIRE BAY.

Among the finest carriage horses in the world is the high-class Yorkshire Bay, combining as he does the quality and grace of the Thoroughbred with the strength, color and beauty of form of the Cleveland. He is an ideal of all that is magnificent and useful in the carriage horse. His color is a rich, shining bay; his coat is as bright and fine and as glossy and as iridescent as that of the race horse; his legs, mane and tail are raven black, setting off the splendor of his golden color. He is strong and lengthy; he stands over a great deal of ground; his top has the flowing lines of the Cleveland back and level quarter; his ribs are well sprung; he carries his neat head and arched crest, as well as his high-set tail, with all the pride and grace of an Arab, and no bearing-rein is needed to make him bend. At rest and in action he is a golden picture of stateliness. There may be other breeds that lift the knee higher, but the movement of the Yorkshire Bay is fine and free; it is not a mere snapping of the knee and flexing of the hocks, but he moves smoothly, evenly and with liberty from the shoulders and thighs; stepping lightly and airily, yet with a long reach, he covers the ground swiftly and with ease.

The Yorkshire Bay is a created type. Its home is the north and east ridings of Yorkshire. It has been formed by selection and crossing the Cleveland directly or indirectly with the Thoroughbred.

THE FRENCH COACH

horses are a combination of power, endurance and elegance
that represents the outcome of centuries of government protection, and the careful breeding of the best horses obtainable,
controlled by the best minds trained for the purpose and sup-
ported by unlimited means. No other civilized nation has
ever taken the uninterrupted interest in the improvement of
the equine race that France has evinced. As early as the
feudal ages her stock of horses had a far-reaching fame, due
to the individual necessity of the knight. As the government
became more centralized, the powers of State became responsible for the production of a higher class of horses for military
protection and equipment. As early as 1690, statistics prove
France to have had 1600 horses in her federal studs. A
century later this number had increased to 3239 stallions
that sired 55,000 living colts. From 1815 to 1833 France
bought 1902 stallions for public service, and of these 223
came from Arabia and other foreign countries. The remainder were selections principally within her own borders.
In 1833 a royal stud-book was established, and since then
the improvement in horses has been greater than ever. The
Government has kept one central object constantly in view—
to encourage the people by every possible means to a higher
standard of breeding, and at the same time to furnish them
the means by which to accomplish this purpose, by introdu-
cing in every locality the finest of the different breeds and
types, which are offered for service to owners of choice mares
at nominal fees. The animals mentioned are not all owned
by the Government, but many are owned by individuals, and
having been inspected and approved by the authorized offi-
cials, are employed at 300 to 3000 francs per annum, and
others still, though not salaried, are recommended govern-
mentally as worthy of public patronage. To prevent the use

of inferior stock, all horses not authorized by Government are excluded from service. Besides this, large sums are annually expended as prizes for choice colts reared under governmental auspices.

STANDARDBRED HORSES.

A Thoroughbred horse is usually understood to be a running horse, while a Standardbred is one bred to trot. America

RYSDYCK'S HAMBLETONIAN.

and Russia are the only two countries where that artificial gait, the trot, has been bred for and highly developed. The importation of the thoroughbred Messenger, in 1788, was the beginning of an interest in trotting in this country and Canada. To-day almost every American trotting horse traces his pedigree back to old Messenger, who was foaled in 1780, and who in turn was descended from Darley's Arabian. Messenger was gray, and was 15.3 hands high. He was an animal of great vigor and soundness, and was a natural trotter. He was the great grandsire of Hambletonian, of whom an illustration is given taken from a photograph. Hambletonian is the founder of the greatest trotting family the world has ever seen. He was foaled May 5, 1849, and died March 27, 1876, and was a beautiful bay, with white hind feet and a small white star in his forehead. His excellence consisted in his long trotting gait, his muscular development and the quality of his sinews and bones. He was never engaged in any race.

The leading families of Standardbred horses are the Hambletonians just referred to; the Membrinos, whose modern head was Mambrino Chief, a descendant of Messenger; the Bashaws, the Clays, the Stars, the Blue Bulls, the Canadians, the Royal Georges, and several Morgan families, to which a section of the chapter is devoted.

THE MORGAN.

The Morgan is termed by many the "American Hackney." He is known as a stayer. The ambition among old Norfolk trotter enthusiasts was not to go a mile in two minutes, but an unlimited distance in a limited time. The aim was 100 miles in ten hours to saddle, and the Morgan has the ability. Circumstances of locality have influenced this breed for such a purpose more than any other class of horses. The hills of New England prevent stretches of speed, and encourage staying powers against adverse conditions. The old Morgan appears to have had size and contour similar to the old Norfolk, with greater substance. For long, steady, untiring work, the Morgan will unquestionably come to the front again in popularity.

The history of the breed dates back to the foaling of Justin Morgan, in 1793. This horse was taken from his home at

Springfield, Mass., when two years old, to Vermont. He was dark bay, fourteen hands, and 950 pounds. His walk was rapid and trot a smooth stride, and he was noted for courage, untiring action and beauty. Justin Morgan is conceded to have much Arabian blood in him. He left six entire sons—Hawkins, Sherman, Bulrush, Fenton, Revenge and Woodbury. Sherman, Bulrush and Woodbury left stock

OLD ETHAN ALLEN.

that has made them famous. From the first came the Black horses : Ethan Allens, Lamberts, Knoxes and Herods ; from Bulrush the Morrils and Fearnaughts, and from Woodbury the Golddusts and Magna Chartas. The Morgan is a trotting roadster, only that instead of turning off a fast mile he rapidly covers many miles with ease. His animation and eagerness make him a general favorite, whether for pleasure or business. The Morgans are a long-lived race. Justin died at 29, Sherman and Gifford at 26, Revenge at 22, Bulrush at 35, Billy Root at 23 and Royal at 37.   Their prepotency for 100 years has been remarkable.   The illustration shows Ethan Allen, one of the famous descendants of Justin Morgan.

THE HACKNEY.

Many persons make the mistake of believing every compactly-built horse a Hackney, when in truth this animal is a

THE HACKNEY.

distinctly English-bred trotter of exact type and antiquity of origin, dating, his lovers say, as far back in English literature as 1170.   A Hackney should be bred for quality as much as possible, and he must have bone and muscle enough to do the work required of him.   The demand is for power enough to draw four persons ten to twelve miles per hour without trouble. The Hackney has made some remarkable records as a trotter, and his courage and intelligence make him an aristocrat among horses. Just at present the fad of fashion seems to have turned his way, and probably one-half the horses exhibited in the great horse shows of the country are Hackneys. Their compact build, bright eye and high knee action make them sought after for the carts and carriages of the rich.

THE DRAUGHT HORSE—THE FARMER'S HORSE.

Few men who buy horses will ask whether they are Norman, Clyde, Belgian, Percheron or Suffolk. They only

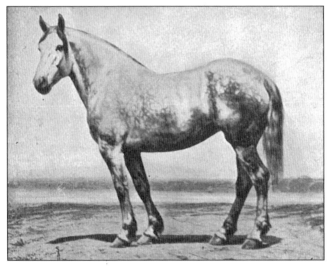

PERCHERON BROOD MARE.

seek large, handsome, good horses, reasonably sound, with free action, and will pay good money and be glad to get them. They are all grand horses, and except for the heavily haired leg, or clean leg, no man can tell one from another. All are most valuable and come from one source.

They have become what we see them by climatic influence, feed and environment. We must have weight to suit the city markets. A proud-stepping, vigorous, powerful Draught Horse, with beautiful form, is eagerly demanded by commerce. Only high-class mares and the best Draught sires can produce such horses. Too many small chunks are bred.

They fail to bring Draught-Horse prices, and their breeders then pronounce Draught-Horse breeding a failure.

A requisite for the farmer's horse is early maturity, or size and strength to perform much of the farmer's necessary work while growing or being fitted for market, and this without breaking

HEAD OF DRAUGHT HORSE.

down or being injured in any way by such work.

He should be of medium size, evenly proportioned, with flat limbs powerfully jointed, but not coarse. Bays, browns and chestnuts are the favorite colors.

Select animals with a swinging road gait that will draw two men a mile in four minutes, or ten miles an hour—a horse that can go fifty to sixty miles in a day without feeling it. The action should be courageous and free, and he should have bottom enough to repeat the performance as frequently as one may desire. It is not difficult to get a high price for such horses. The man who has any Hackneys, French Coachers, or Cleveland Bays, is not far out of the way.

There is no brighter possibility for the farmer than in breeding large, young native mares of amiable disposition to full-blood stallions, thus obtaining half-blood grades at slight cost. Such animals are as good for all practical uses as if full-bloods, and sell as well for all purposes except breeding.

Why does not some enterprising breeder make a specialty of intelligence in horses, as has been done in the case of the

CLYDESDALE.

dog with marvelous results? There would be money in the thing.

Let the breeder of horses school himself to sell his stock for just what it is. He will quickly make a good name for himself, and be able to get for his really good horses enough to more than recompense what he loses in telling the truth about the poorer ones.

A good riding horse should have a long neck and carry its head high. The rider wants to see some horse ahead of him.

THE GOOD MULE.

" It is a poor mule that won't work both ways."

Having made a business of rearing mules for market, I have learned many things concerning the breeding and usefulness of this animal that those persons should have who are convinced he is a vicious and untrustworthy brute.

To breed anything like the ideal mule, greater care must be exercised in the selection of sire and dam than is necessary in producing a model horse. How many ill-shaped, ugly mules we see, each the result of careless breeding! I have been taught by observation that more depends upon the sire than upon the dam in getting an ideal mule foal. Good points, however, come readily from both sides. Some men, in selecting a Jack, look to his height, and, for such, the more daylight found under him the better. What foolish men! The Jack must be low and heavily quartered, with large bone and a neat head. This sire will bring good mules nearly every time. Some men who own curby, heavy crooked mares say, "They'll do to raise mules." This carelessness, coupled with ignorance, accounts for the great number of degenerated hybrids.

A mule possesses keener instinct than a horse, and for this reason is easily trained. He should be handled from the very beginning of his life. A small leather halter should be worn about the stable for the purpose of holding him while being patted and rubbed about the head. This kind treatment will win respect for the owner of the most stubborn little hybrid for all future time. I have never found an exception to this rule. I have found, however, that by tickling and teasing, it is easy to get an all-round kicker. The young mule should be bitted when rising in his second year, and harnessed to light work. I have never seen a mule that I could not train to be good and gentle by handling him firmly, but easily and quietly. A good, tough mule will usually show

TIM'S TEAM.

it when a stranger approaches him. He will be shy. This shyness is his staple virtue, and means snap.

What is the mule best adapted to? and what is he not adapted to? I use mules only on my farm and have no horses. The mule is harnessed for all purposes, from plow·

ing in new ground to attending funerals—both solemn occasions. He has a swinging gait, peculiar to himself, that makes him a speedy animal for such farm work as mowing and raking, cultivating and reaping. He is especially well adapted to the coach, being sufficiently speedy and exceedingly plucky, and handsome enough for any king to sit behind. General George Washington, much noted for keeping handsome horses, was also an extensive raiser of mules. Among the hills of Pennsylvania, where lumbering and mining is so extensively carried on, the mule is king of the collar. In this county (Westmoreland) the mule market is always good. I am happy to say the tariff never affects our mule market very much. Among the mountains of Western Pennsylvania the mule is an indispensable beast, as much as on the cotton and tobacco plantations, and in the cane brakes of the sunny South.

Speaking of mules, Rufus Mason says: To a young man courting a girl whom he suspects is not quite as sensible as she ought to be, he can go on horseback; but the day after the wedding, trade off the horses and get a first-rate mule team. She won't dress so fine to ride behind mules; and, seeing that the mules are sensible and businesslike, she will have a good example before her.

SHETLAND PONY.

The Shetland ponies are from thirty-four to forty-four inches high. They are very hardy and strong, with long manes and tails. These are a protection to them in the cold climate in which they are reared. They have long and shaggy coats. After being in America a few years their coats become finer. The Shetland Islands, where they come from, are north of Scotland. The pasture is scanty, and the climate severe. This is why they have become so small.

They will carry a full-grown man, but the trouble is to find a good place for the rider's feet. But they are just adapted to the boy and girl.

A child will get more fun, physical development, and ruddy health to the square inch with a pony, than in any other way. The child who has a pony should be taught to care for it. In this way the little boy or girl can take in horse sense, and this knowledge of how to do things will be

A FRIEND OF THE BOYS AND GIRLS.

of great benefit to them. The pony will think more of them and they will think more of the pony. There is now a great demand for ponies, and there will be more as people find out how much good it is for the children to own them.

The picture represents Sparkle, a beautiful specimen owned by J. Murray Hoag, of Maquoketa, Iowa, who imports large numbers of them.

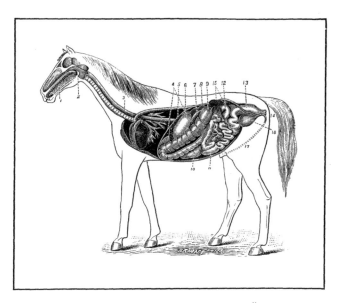

SHOWING DIGESTIVE APPARATUS.*

1. Mouth.
2. Pharynx.
3. Œsophagus.
4. Diaphragm.
5. Spleen.
6. Stomach.
7. Duodenum.
8. Liver, upper extremity.
9. Large colon.
10. Cæcum.
11. Small intestine.
12. Floating colon.
13. Rectum.
14. Anus.
15. Left kidney and its ureter.
16. Bladder.
17. Urethra.

* Haines, after Megnin. From Prof. Michener in U. S. Gov.
Report on Diseases of Animals.

CHAPTER II.

FEEDING AND WATERING.

Observations on Feeding—Rules for Watering—Salting—
Feeding Conveniences and Watering Tank and Trough—
General Notes.

> *Of food and drink give me the best,*
> *From brutal treatment keep me free;*
> *Give me when tired a little rest,*
> *And see how useful I can be.*

A horse has a smaller stomach than an ox and consequently it must be fed less at a time. It has less power to
digest coarse foods. It eats much slower, as it must do all
its chewing before the food is swallowed. For these reasons
it requires a longer time to eat and its food should be more
concentrated. It wants only a little coarse food at a time.

Most people feed too much rather than too little. Two
pounds per day of hay and grain for each 100 pounds of live
weight, is usually enough for good working condition. A
general all-round good ration for any horse consists of six
parts bran, three of oats and one of linseed-oil meal. It is a
grand combination for muscle, for work and for health. In
cold weather corn should be added, and the cornmeal, oats
and bran may be of equal weight, still adding a little linseed
meal. Feed a small amount of hay twice a day.

There is no doubt that farmers generally depend too much
on corn to feed their work horses. Corn is good to lay on
fat, but muscle is what a work horse needs, to give which

oats are a much better feed. However plentiful corn may be, it should be fed sparingly. Lay on as much muscle as you please, the more the better, but a horse overburdened with fat is unable to stand as much hard work as one whose muscles are better developed.

Great care and regularity should be given to watering and feeding. The water should in summer be clean, fresh and cool, and in the winter should be free from ice. Every horse should have cut hay, straw, corn-fodder, or wheat chaff, wetted and mixed with bran, at least once a day the year round. In the hot weather a horse should not be fed much corn. Bran and oats are much better. The more work the more feed, of course.

The practice of feeding the horse when tired and thirsty is altogether too common, and then too with the extra thirst of a full meal allow it to gorge itself with water. When this is done the horse should remain quiet for a full hour before starting on the road or at hard work to get space for its lungs to play and its heart to beat, by the digestion of the food and its removal to the bowels.

Did you ever get in your mouth or on your plate some potato that had soured in the hot weather? If so, you know something of the misery a horse must suffer when compelled to take all his food from a sour manger. Cut food, moistened, is very likely to sour the manger. The good horseman will always bend over it when tying his charges. Sourness is easily detected and easily cured by a pail of scalding water. A pinch of charcoal dust thrown in the manger daily will help keep things sweet and prevent acidity in the horse's stomach.

If the horse eats lots of grain and does not do well, it must have sore teeth or a poor digestion. It is an easy thing to have the teeth smoothed so it can eat well. If the trouble is in the stomach, feed less grain. Too much grain will often make a disordered stomach, and the animal will do better on less.

The breath of a horse or any other animal upon its food is unwholesome. For this reason put into the manger only food enough for one meal.

Meal is not a natural food for a horse which can chew well. They eat it too fast and it does not get enough saliva with it to digest well. The saliva is the first secretion in the process of digestion and it must do its part to have the food agree fully with the animal.

Green forage crops must be fed with discretion and not largely at first, or the result will be profuse sweating, resulting in weakness, and sometimes colic. It is never safe to turn horses with strong, unsatisfied appetites for green crops loose in the rank growth.

Every barn should have a bran bin which should be replenished annually at the time when bran is low in price. Its cost per ton is usually as low or lower than that of the best hay. Bran should be fed liberally when the old coat is shedding, and each horse should be treated to a daily ration in summer. Its tendency is laxative, keeping the entire system cool, and its effect upon the skin excellent, preventing surface irritation common among animals fed largely upon corn. Four quarts of bran with a pint to a quart of oil meal lightly salted will appeal keenly to the horse's taste.

Potatoes are an excellent food for horses during the winter, in connection with other food, keeping their bowels open and their skins loose.

There is nothing better than sweet apples to help put a horse in fine condition. Give them four quarts at a mess three times a day with the grain. Few people realize the value of sweet apples as a relish for horses.

One of the most useful foods whether green or hayed is oats and peas. The crop is easily raised in large quantities op rich land well prepared, where one-half bushel of peas ars sown with two and one-half bushels of oats per acre. As soon as the peas are in full bloom the fodder is ready for use, and all should be cut for feeding or drying before the peas are ripe. If it should happen to be dull weather and the crop matures, no harm has been done, because it can be cured, run through the threshing machine and straw cutter, moistened, and the ground oats and peas sprinkled over it.

Experienced horsemen understand that with a heavy feed of oats, at night, and a light breakfast, a horse gets a reserved stock of muscular strength laid in in advance, and travels faster and further than one having a hearty morning feed.

A warm bran mash does good occasionally. Don't let the bowels of any horse become constipated.

A night pasture for work horses will help to cool their blood. Give them their grain ration just the same.

There are a few horses whose stomachs will not tolerate rye in any form ; will either get colic or staggers. Rye is always a dangerous feed when given alone.

Spasmodic salting is all wrong for any animal, and especially for horses. It may cause colic, and often does. The horse eats too much salt at a time, if only salted now and then, and when this is the case the coats of the stomach and the bowels are irritated, and congestion takes place and excessive thirst. The horse then drinks too much and a chill follows, and this makes more congestion and inflammation may follow, and colic and a set-back, if not death. What is the use of such doings ? It is just as easy, and easier, to be more sensible, and to keep salt before the horse all the time, and then it will partake as directed by its instincts, and only a lick will be eaten. Prepare the horse for the constant supply by giving it a little every day for a week, and then no harm will come.

Teamsters should feed their own horses, and every teamster who takes pride in his team should handle the measure himself, and should make appetite and digestion of food a subject of study.

Horses refuse their feed because of overwork, too little exercise, or because the food is not right in some way, soreness of mouth or teeth, or general faulty management. If the trouble is due to overfeeding, short rations for a day or two will remedy it. Food that is not eaten within a reasonable time should be removed from the manger and the ration correspondingly reduced. No animal should have more than he will eat up clean. When a horse refuses to eat and becomes thin and weak for no apparent reason, he should have some condiment to increase the appetite. A good combination is the following : Ground oats and corn, of each five pounds ; oil meal, four ounces; salt, two ounces ; a dessertspoonful of powdered gentian, and a small teaspoonful of dried sulphate of iron. If the animal refuses the ration a little starvation will make him taste it, when his dislike will cease at once. Begin with a small quantity of this mixture for each meal, and increase it gradually until a full ration is being fed.

Water your horse before you give him hay. Give him hay before you give him grain. Give the concentrated food last. His stomach is not large enough to hold all at once.

The digestion of food is frequently badly retarded or prevented by mistakes in watering. Water should always be offered the horse twenty minutes before he is fed, and never less than two hours after feeding. The drink is rapidly taken from the stomach by the intestines, and the time mentioned is sufficient to distribute three or four gallons of water throughout the digestive tract, diluting the salivary secretion so as to supply all water needed for digestion of the food. When regular watering is practiced no water will be craved soon after food. To observe this method prevents the washing of undigested food from the stomach into the intestines, where it ferments, producing gas and resulting in colic.

THE BARN TANK.

There is no greater convenience in and about a horse barn than water obtainable instantly and at wholesale. Many

 persons are not situated where they can have pipe water at command, and will delight in arranging a tank in the upper part of the barn which may be kept full by the use of a hand or power pump. This tank should have an overflow pipe so that it will never be filled so full as to make trouble. It need not be anything more than a cask well hooped and painted. A 100-gallon box lined with metal will answer better, perhaps, in quickly supplying drink for the horses, water for sponging their feet and legs, washing carriages, washing the floors and windows, etc. A hose is a great aid to the rapid washing of windows, and with a tank in the loft one is as independent of city water works as of Niagara. In connection with the water system every one should have a slatted platform an inch or two above the ground, where the wagons may be drawn for washing. Here the water and mud are instantly washed away, so that the hands and sponge are kept clean avoiding varnish scratching, and the feet are not kept in a puddle.

The most economical troughs are those made from plank. Use *pine* plank two inches thick. The plank must contain no knots or wind shakes, nor large cracks. The excellence of this sort of a trough especially depends upon the way in

FIG. 1.

which it is made. Two drawings will show best and quickest the right and the wrong way. Letting one part into another makes the trough tighter, and if let in as shown in Fig. 1, and not as shown in Fig. 2, the trough will be made much stronger and more durable. The bottom is let into the sides also. Smooth the edges to be let in. Lay them against the plank to be grooved, make a mark close to each edge, and then saw just a little inside of each mark, so the groove is a little narrower than the edge to be fitted in it. Saw a long quarter of an inch deep and then chip out the wood with a chisel, making the groove of the same depth throughout. Paint the groove and edge with thick paint—brown mineral paint is cheapest and best—before they are put together. As Fig. 1 does not show the end piece let into the bottom, the reader is safe in concluding that the better way is to let the end of the bottom into the end piece. The bolts should be of iron, one-half inch in diameter. With

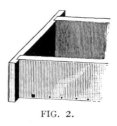

FIG. 2.

the grooves they will hold the trough well together, and no nails should be used. Such a trough is durable. Bore a hole in the bottom of every trough and fit it with a hardwood plug. Then the water can be let out of freezing nights. If a stout tarred string is tied to the end of the

plug and fastened to the top of the trough, the plug will
not be lost, and one will not have sometimes to reach into
cold water to pull out the plug.   It pays to have plenty
of good troughs about the farm.

The horse that eats his grain too hastily is sure, sooner or
later, to become a dyspeptic.   Bolted food cannot be assim-
ilated, and hence is worse than wasted, as it deranges and
poisons the digestive organs.   Some horses, whose stomachs
are already out of order more or less, from the vice of
too eager eating, will plunge their noses into the oats nearly
to the eyes, fill their mouths and fairly crowd the food
down their own throats.   To prevent disease is always better

than endeavors to cure it.   Realizing
this truth many a horse owner has tried
in various ways to force a slow consump-
tion of food in his stables.   Some spread
the oats in the bottom of a large manger;
others keep a peck of small stones there,
from between which the horse is compelled to pick his food.   Good horsemen
of New York state have widely adopted the slow delivery
chute.   It is built into the manger, as the cut shows, and
reaches to within half an inch of its bottom.   A metal
manger should be used, or a wooden one lined with tin or
iron, as a greedy horse will destroy it by gnawing because
dissatisfied with rational eating.   Colts brought up at such
mangers will rarely become gourmands afterwards, and are
doubly valuable because so seldom out of condition, with
resultant colic, etc.

It is a waste of time and increase of trouble to go into the
loft whenever the horses are to be fed.   It is convenient and
economical to cut a week's supply of hay at one time, say
during a shower or when a change of work is desired.

The hay is not thrown down haphazard to create a dust all through the barn and set the horses coughing, but is cut into

a chute, made dust tight with putty. This is located under the stairs in one corner out of the way, and a slope bottom renders every ounce of the cut hay easily available. To prevent clogging and increase the storage capacity, the chute was built larger at the bottom than at the top.

READY FOR BREAKFAST.

Chapter III.

IN THE STABLE AND AT WORK.

The Stable Should Be Light, Clean and Free from Bad
Odors ; the Floor Even—Grooming—Bedding—Conven-
iences — The Good Teamster — Overloading — Trotting
Down Hill.

> *Feed me on good oats and hay,*
> *Give me drink three times a day ;*
> *In the pasture let me play,*
> *Groom me well, for it will pay.*

A good horseman cannot be too careful about his stable.
It should be well ventilated, scrupulously clean, well drained,

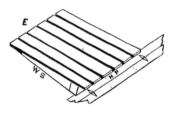

and have low mangers and
a floor that never gets out
of true from wearing by the
shoes or settling of the
building. There is no floor
that is better than plank,
all things considered, but
it should not slope too
much from front to rear, as is often the case.

It is well to have the floor supplemented by a lower floor
which has a more decided slope, the surface floor to consist
of two to three-inch planks one-half to three-quarters of an
inch apart, held in place by cleats or iron rods. This surface floor may be leveled up by resting on a thick cross-
piece at the rear and a very thin one or none at all forward.
The perfect stable floor should stop one foot or more short of

the manger, where the horse's fore feet come when he is
feeding.   This space should be filled with earth, which is
beneficial in cooling the feet, keeping the frogs healthy, and
which he will paw to a level he finds most restful.

The sub-floor must have a decided slope and be cleaned
often by raising the level surface floor and sifting dry earth
through it.

Another good floor is made of solid concrete, two inches
higher forward than back.   On this is a slat floor for the animals to stand upon.   The slats are four inches thick at the
rear and only two inches thick forward, thus making the
floor level.   The planks cover the gutter, making the stable
neat in every respect.

The stable must be light or the eyes will be injured.   The
air must be pure or the lungs will be impaired.   A foul
stable will sicken the horses.   The horse stables should be
cleaned every day.   Use plenty of plaster to absorb the
ammonia, and see that the ventilation is good and that there
are no draughts.

It will certainly injure the horse's eyes to take it from a
dark stable into the glare of sunlight reflected from snow.
The injury may be slight, and it may be serious.   If repeated, it may make the horse blind.   The remedy is a light
stable.   A light stable—made so by glass windows—is more
healthy than a dark one.

Sometimes slight settling of the barn will slope the stall
floors toward the manger, or make them so level that urine
will cause trouble.   Besides rendering the horse more difficult to keep clean, the ammonia generated
will be a dangerous admixture in the air
for the animal's lungs and eyes.

Any person who has used a scraper like
the one shown in the engraving will never be without one.   It

is merely a 2-foot board edged with hoop iron and fastened to a brace and handle. After thoroughly shaking up and removing the bedding no shovel will so quickly scrape out the stable.

Soaked bedding it is necessary to dry each day, especially in village stables. There is nothing that will so quickly ac-

complish the purpose as the frame and wheelbarrow shown. Bedding may be placed upon this two inches deep, wheeled into the sun and wind and dried in an hour, as the wind penetrates it from below as well as on all sides. All that is necessary is a sound wheel. Pieces of scantling firmly nailed together improvise the remainder of the contrivance.

A good hook for the harness may be made of a piece of inch and a half oak plank three inches wide and eighteen inches long. Six inches from one end a hole should be bored by which it is screwed to the side of the post or other upright. Near the outer edge of this beam a cleat should be nailed, on which the oak stick may rest when turned down. A heavy nail driven over its rear end will also help steady it if the weight be heavy. Of course, the holder may be shaped as neatly as one desires. When not in use it may be turned up out of the way.

Careful and thorough grooming is almost as essential as feeding and cannot be dispensed with profitably. Many who care for their own horses detest the work, but largely because they do not do it in the easiest way, which is the most systematic.

Procure a well-made, rice-root brush, and with this in one hand and a currycomb in the other, start the job at the horse's head on the near side.   Never use the comb on head, mane nor tail.   Carefully brush the left side of the head until it is clean and shiny.   Then proceed to the neck, thence to the shoulders, using the comb now to loosen up the hair and dirt, and only advancing as the portion under consideration is thoroughly cleansed and beautified.   Before touching the body scrape, brush, clean and smooth the left side of both forward legs.   When all of this side has been well groomed down to the last hair of both hind feet, the tail must be carefully and persistently brushed.   This done, proceed to the right side of the head and follow the formula given for the left side.   If the head is difficult to groom satisfactorily, rub the hair the wrong way with the brush and then smooth it.   This will soon conquer the worst case and do it agreeably to the horse.

Be gentle with the horses.   Nervous excitement deranges the digestive organs.   Worry the horse by voice or whip and he will be thin, no matter what you feed him.   Even a horse appreciates a musical voice, with a kind intonation.

In cleaning horses after coming in from work, or in the morning, if the floor back of your stalls is large enough to clean horses in, they should be cleaned there in preference to the stall.   Put a screw-eye in the wall up as high as you can reach, tie a hitch rein with a snap to it ; right opposite to this, in the stall post, put another screw-eye or screw ring, lead your horse out and snap the hitch rein in the side ring of the halter, then tie the halter rein in the ring opposite.   You can get around him without trouble, and if he should happen to be a biter, he can't get at you.

After going over his body with currycomb, take a common broom and brush all the dust off of him you can.   It will take out lots of dust in a short time.   If your comb is new and teeth sharp, run a file over them a few times.

After brushing, take a cloth and go over him from head to heel, pick out his feet with an article like this, called a foot hook (one side is a hook about an inch and a half long, the other chisel-shaped), and he is ready to go to his stall. Horse's feet should be examined every day. The second illustration is called a scraper, for taking off sweat  or mud. It is made of hard wood about a foot long, one inch wide, sharp edges and slightly bent near the end. An old piece of grass matting is a good thing to take mud off the legs with.

To dispose of your horse's foretop, if heavy, try parting in the middle before putting on the bridle.

Fetlocks may catch and hold mud and ice and be harder to clean than clipped ankles, but certainly they keep off wind and prevent direct contact of ice with the skin; therefore, don't bare the ankles. If frozen in tags they may be cleaned and dried quickly by dipping in hot water and sawing with an old sack. It is easier and more speedy than rubbing. The heat produced will leave the fetlocks dry.

The old feed bag, too full of holes to be worth mending, is good for nothing, eh? Saw the wet and muddy legs of the tired horse with it, and see how dry and clean they will become. The labor isn't great, but the results are.

No brush will take the dust out of a horse's coat and make it glisten like a stiff broom in the hands of a strong, energetic man. Its handle must be cut off to two feet. It seems to afford sufficient leverage so considerable power may be brought to bear on the coat.

During the shedding season, use only an old and dull currycomb. A sharp one will inflict pain, a thing the humane person will avoid.

There is nothing so sweet, clean, and economical for the horse's bed as sawdust, where straw is too expensive.   Tan bark and sawdust mixed also make a good bed.

Never tie a horse so long that he can put his head on the floor.   If he can put his head down he is likely to roll and get cast.

To get horses from a burning barn or stable, when panic-stricken, put the harness on them and they can then be easily and safely removed.   If no harness is at hand one's coat or blanket thrown over his head makes him tractable.

The way to hang the lantern in the stable is to stretch a wire tight overhead far enough behind the horses to be out of the way, and to attach a hook to this wire on which the lantern is hung—and have the hook so loose that it will slide along easily.   When this is done, the lantern will not be upset, and danger from fire will be lessened.

Do not get it into your head that a man can work a team and take the right kind of care of them, or anywhere near it, and do a lot of chores, say milk nine or ten cows, feed and water fifteen or twenty hogs, cut all the wood, etc., and whoever expects it is very apt to be disappointed.   That is, when the team is doing hard work every day that is usual on a farm in the busy season.

The intelligent reader will not be slow to see the advantages of the idea of the illustration herewith.   The horse or colt that is accustomed to getting cast in the stall, can be prevented from doing so by the use of a strap fastened to a joist overhead, so that the animal cannot get its head quite down to  the floor.   This device is necessary in some cases, and is effective.

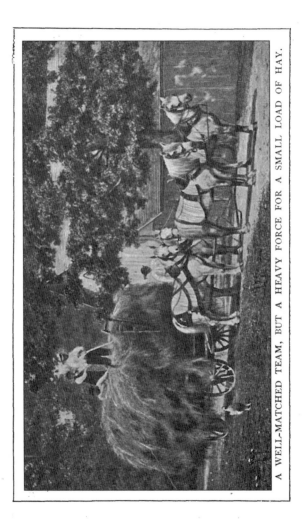

A WELL-MATCHED TEAM, BUT A HEAVY FORCE FOR A SMALL LOAD OF HAY.

There is a great difference in methods of managing horses to get from them the best and longest service. Some men invariably drive rapidly, regardless of the condition of roads; others not only drive with consideration, but continually guide the team so that the wagon will avoid all stones and heavy ruts, making it a constant endeavor to husband the resources of the horses. Rapid, careless, and often inhuman driving will wear out the best pair of horses in one-half the time they will serve efficiently and profitably in the hands of a rational man.

Don't be deceived into believing that because you own a horse you may treat him as you choose, no matter how cruelly. To such a statement every impulse of merciful humanity rises in opposition. Every State Humane Society remonstrates, and has the arm of strong law on its side. The penalties for abuse are heavy. And it is right.

Better go twice than to overload the team. This over-loading is a most frightful cause of unsoundness. When loaded, stop often. It pays.

There are lots of fools who drive horses, and one of the biggest is the one who makes the horse trot down hill. It hurts the horse, as it jars the shoulders, and may bring paralysis of the muscles and nerves and to cause sweeny, or shoulder soreness. It also weakens the tendons and "springs" the knees, and then the animal cannot stand erect on its fore feet or hold back down hill. There is always more danger in going fast down hill if anything gives away. A horse should always be taught to go carefully down hill, and not pellmell.

Make haste slowly for the first mile or two when starting out for a drive. Try it, and see how much easier and more satisfactorily your horse will accomplish whatever is required of him.

Do the horses seem to sweat easily at their work in the spring? They are not hard yet. Be easy with them for a few days. As Pat says: "Be aisy; and if ye can't be aisy, be as aisy as ye can."

Don't let the colts and young horses get discouraged with heavy loads. Better go a few more times, or hire in a day's work, than to spoil a promising team.

When your horse is heated from riding or driving do not let him stand in a draught, and, if very warm, rub him briskly all over with a coarse towel or wisp of straw and cover him with a light blanket, which will absorb the perspiration and prevent a chilling of the surface.

Never whip a horse when he is frightened. Be cool yourself and he will soon gain confidence.

The nippy air of winter makes the horses frisky. After the confinement of the stable they want to go. If a rein should break their going might be serious. Perhaps the sewing of some of the splices has begun to give way. Better see about it.

Bring the horse up to the hitching post with his head from the wind. He will not get so cold as if his head is toward the wind, and he will stand better. The horse will stand more quietly while you are hitching him if his head is from the wind.

HORSE MAXIMS.

TIM says:

The nervous horse should have less oats and more bran.

The collar must not be too wide nor too short.

It does a horse a wonderful amount of good to rub its legs a few minutes after a hard drive, with a woolen cloth.

Give the horses a few potatoes in their feed occasionally. They are good for horses and bad for worms.

The blanket is for outside the stable, not in it. If the horse in the stable is so cold as to need a blanket, he should be given a better stable, and not a blanket. When a horse has free access to salt it seldom has colic and very rarely is troubled with bots.

Cultivate a cheery way of speaking to your horse. Some horses that are cross and lazy, because growled at and punched in the ribs until sour and discouraged, will prick forward their ears and follow them in a hearty, glad manner that is surprising when they are kindly and encouragingly urged.

If a horse eats his bedding use sawdust or fine tan bark.

Don't draw your hames too close at the top; better have them wide so as not to pinch the horse's neck.

Chapter IV.

WHIMS AND VICES.

Managing the Balky Horse—Tail-rubbing—Kicking—The Puller — Pawing — Rolling in the Stable — Tearing the Blanket.

For a balky horse the only persuaders that should be allowed are the spade and post. They should be carried in the wagon and the spade made to set the post at the horse's head wherever he makes his first stand. Here he should be firmly tied without unharnessing and left until thoroughly tired of standing. If he will not go on then without the whip he should be left several hours more, always without food or drink until he finds he is punishing himself, which almost any horse of intelligence will conclude after standing from thirty to thirty-six hours. When the poor beast does start amiably, he should be praised and petted without stint. After a horse has reached twelve years of age, and perhaps balked and been abused for it most of this time, it may be doubtful if he can be reformed.

Some teamsters start a balky horse by taking him from the wagon and making him turn around in a short circle until giddy. If he doesn't go after the first dance of this sort repeat the process.

To cure a horse of rubbing his tail, wash the dock with warm water and good yellow soap (not soft soap), and thor-

oughly well dry the part with a clean coarse rubber; the
rubbing to be kept up until the part is not only dry, but well
warm with the friction. Also inject a little sweet oil into
the rectum. Then apply a liniment made of new milk and
spirits of turpentine, in the proportion of an ounce of the latter to eight ounces of the former.

If the horse kicks the sides of the stall he can probably be
broken of the habit by hanging a smooth stick of wood from
the joist above by a rope, so that when he indulges his vice,
his feet or legs will strike the stick. This will put it in motion; it will swing back and forth and take his attention so
he will forget about kicking. This is a pretty sure cure.

There is no escape for the puller tied in the following
manner, and the tie will in time break the bad habit: Make
a slip-noose of a strong manilla rope and place it around the
animal just forward of the hind legs, having the noose on
the under side. Then pass the rope between the body and
girt, next between the forward legs and through the halter
ring and post and tie to the girt. After the puller has set
back on this novel tie once or twice he will find he is only
squeezing himself unpleasantly and that without breaking a
halter or doing any damage.

If the horse paws in the stable, turn it out every day for a
run in a yard. When driven every day it will not paw, unless fed irregularly.

If you cannot stop your horse bolting his food by putting
a handful of shelled corn in his manger, give him cut hay
with ground feed. He will masticate that.

To prevent a horse from rolling in the stable: Fasten a
strap to the ceiling above his shoulders, letting the lower end
hang about two and one-half feet from the ground. Fasten
a ring to the top of the halter, put a snap on the end of the
strap, and snap into the ring. Simple but safe.

To prevent a horse from tearing the blanket with his teeth, a leather shield, as shown in the picture, is sewed to the halter which does not interfere with the animal eating, but does with

its habit of tearing its blanket. The shield should extend four inches below the nose.

The habit of *shying* may come from timidity or defective eyesight. If the latter, it cannot be entirely cured; if the former, gentleness and good sense in the driver will in a great measure overcome the difficulty. Never whip a shying horse past the object which frightens it. This only confirms the habit. Go slow; let the horse have time to see the object and learn that it will not hurt him.

A very bad habit in a horse is that of *sudden starting* when harnessed, and often leads to broken traces, swingle-trees, and to runaways and smashups. The fault is usually taught the horse by a fool driver who cuts him with the whip unexpectedly. A vice of this kind, in a horse that is afraid of the whip, is rarely cured, but may be mitigated by gentleness.

Running away is the worst of vices. Carelessness is the mother of the runaway horse. When the fault is once established it is difficult of cure. All runaways, or horses hard to hold, should be only used with a safety bit, one that will be severe enough to make it painful to attempt to run. By the careful use of such a bit some horses may be gradually cured of the habit of running away.

Chapter V.

HARNESS HINTS.

Halters—The Collar—Blinders—In Fly-time—Triple Reins —Leading a Broncho—A Harness Closet—What Harriet Says.

HALTERS AND HARNESS.

Many a horse is lost or seriously damaged by halters that are unsafe, because weak or improperly constructed. Pullers

are the result of breaking away. A horse that is tied with a halter made like No. 1 will rarely continue to pull. It is like the ordinary halter, excepting that the chin strap is double, and the ring is placed on but half of it. The instant the horse attempts to pull he finds his nose suddenly compressed and

NO. 1.

his breath shut off.

The unpleasant sensation ceases at once when he stands up to the post and behaves himself. This is an effective halter to place on halter-pullers. No. 2 is made of a single piece of rope, can be constructed in five minutes at a cost of five cents, and is extremely handy where one suddenly desires a number of halters for sending away horses that have been sold. It is not a safe night halter, as it is liable to be rubbed off. By attaching a throat strap to it, however, it may be made to serve satisfactorily for some months.

NO. 2.

A safe and neat tie is a good strap or rope, with a snap on one end. Tie the strap to the post, pass the snap through the bit, over the horse's neck, and snap into the same bit-ring. Any attempt to get away draws the bit towards the crest of the neck uncomfortably.

The good road halter is the simple one drawn. The muzzle piece is a slip-noose, and the only other strap goes over the head back of the bridle, so it cannot be worked off. Throughout it is made of inch and a half heavy leather, and pulling only compresses the horse's mouth. It is quickly and easily put on, even with numb hands, and is tasteful for ladies' use. Don't tolerate a road halter with a short tie strap.

Keep the collar clean. Oil it once a month, the rest of the harness twice a year. Clean the leather before you apply the dressing—twice as much neat's-foot oil as beef tallow, with a dash of castor oil, no lampblack. Oil to the harness increases the wear of both it and the horse.

A good plan of haltering horses is shown here. Put a staple on the outside of the manger, put the halter strap through this, and tie the end of the halter to a block of wood below the staple. This will always keep the slack taut.

Take the horse to the harness shop, and do not buy a collar that does not fit. A slight misfit may be overcome by making a cut where it will be covered by the hame and removing some of the padding. The collar will not be injured.

An unnecessarily cruel thing about a harness is a tight throat strap. Don't leave it so loose that the bridle can be rubbed off during fly-time, but see that it does not press the throat when the head is up, thus cutting off the breath, stopping the blood and causing a swelling of the throat glands.

It is cruel to make a horse work in a hard, ill-fitting collar. How do you like a shoe that causes blisters, corns and bunions on your feet?

In the name of all that is humane, dispense with the old flapping blinders that have long ago lost shape and straps to keep them in place. They endanger the sight and are a source of discomfort to the poor beast obliged to submit to such cruelty. Take your jackknife and cut them off.

The only horse that should have the overdraw check rein is the one that is hard-mouthed and pulls on the lines, or the one that continually jerks on the lines to loosen them. Such horses are greatly improved by this rein.

Take the fasteners from an old overshoe and sew or rivet a five-inch strip of leather to the same, and use for horse-tail tie.

In fly-time, put a big crupper pad under the tail of the horse, big enough to raise it up so the animal cannot hug it when it switches over the reins. This is a simple contrivance and a safe one. Put buckles on this big pad and buckle it under the back strap, the same as the regular one. When under the tail, the horse cannot hold the rein.

Here is shown the way that shy bronchos are led behind a wagon in the far West. Take a half-inch rope, lay the two ends together and tie a knot about five feet from the other end

where you see A. ⸱ Now lay it on so that the knot is in
the center of the horse's back and his tail over the rope,
put the ends through the halter ring at C, one rope being on
each side of the neck, and tie the ends together to the wagon.
You may be sure that the animal will lead and not pull
back the wagon.　Horses if tied in this way in narrow stalls
can be cured of halter-pulling.

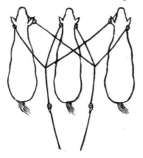

Triple reins are easily made
and are sometimes needed on the
farm.　Have the harness maker
make the extra check lines the
right length ; and then put them
on the buckle of the lines in use
and you have them in good
shape. The ring and snap should
be used on all the lines.　In
driving four horses abreast use
the usual checks on each team, and put a short "jocky
strap" on the inside horses, from bit to bit.

A HARNESS CLOSET.

Few things have a greater tendency to preserve harnesses
than neatness and order, whose prime essentials are careful
cleaning and careful hanging.
No good horseman throws
his harnesses on the floor or
carelessly over a hook in the
open barn or stable.　A tight
closet, where all the harnesses, saddles, sponges, oils,

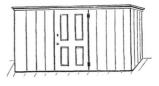

wrenches, and other stable requisites may be kept away from
ammonia, dust and light, is a great economy.　Its first cost
does not need to be great if one possesses an old door.　A

few feet of matched lumber will quickly take the shape of
the closet shown, in almost any part of the barn, if the
manipulator has a little ingenuity. If the lumber is old it
should be liberally puttied and painted. The habit of putting in this closet everything which will make the barn look
untidy will soon give the owner a reputation for neatness, as
well as lightening the drain upon his pocketbook for things
lost or spoiled.

HARRIET BIGGLE says:

*Hang up the halters where they can be found in the dark
on returning from a drive.*

Knots in the traces look bad for the man who ties them.

*Keep the harness strong in every part or there may be a
break away from home, a runaway, and somebody hurt or
possibly killed.*

*Don't try to fit a horse to the collar. It won't work. Fit
the collar to the horse.*

*In oiling harnesses which have been neglected, a better
supply can be put on more quickly, reaching to every rusty
buckle, tongue and crevice, with a small pointed brush, than
with any other appliance.*

Be sure the blinders do not rub the eyes of the horse.

Cover the bits with smooth leather for winter use.

*Spring devices attached to the whiffletrees are very bene-
ficial, especially in plowing stony ground. In their use the
jarring is overcome. Use them on all heavy wagons also.
The horses appreciate them.*

Chapter VI.

AILMENTS AND REMEDIES.

Most Ailments Come from Improper Feeding and Watering
—Importance of Having a Good Teamster—Worms—
Indigestion—Colic—Sore Shoulders—Choking Distemper
—Heaves—Dysentery.

With food don't stuff me, yet stint me not;
Give me water to drink when I am not too hot;
Then come what may, I'll fail you not.

The majority of horse ailments may be traced, directly or
indirectly, to improper feeding and watering, careless management in the stable and in harness.

A careless driver is a very frequent cause of loss. On the
contrary, a driver who is a close observer of the team in his
charge, noting every move made and understanding the animals' requirements and ability, rarely has a sick, lame or
galled horse. For this reason, to place a cheap man over a
good pair of horses is the height of folly. The man getting
one-third more wages, who is a good teamster, which includes the terms "good manager," "close observer," and
"humane," will much more than earn the extra money paid
him in increase of work performed, decrease of grain, medicine and repair bills, and length of the horses' period of
usefulness. There is no reason why a first-class team, six to
eight years old, should not serve continuously and satisfactorily for a term of twelve to sixteen years, if properly protected, fed and looked out for.

If, from improper care or feeding, or from some unavoidable cause, your horse is out of condition, you should dose him with little medicine and much common sense.

The horse that allows himself to be caught lying down may be considered out of condition or lacking sufficient nutritious food. A quart of linseed meal divided into three feeds and added to his grain daily will do him much good and help a quick shedding of the coat.

If a horse cough, dampen his hay, wet his mixed feed, keep him out of a draught ; after exercise blanket him.

Keep hot poultices of bread and milk or oil meal on the neck of horses with throat *Distemper ;* change them often. In severe cases rub the glands and muscles with spirits of turpentine and camphor.

Look out for *Scratches.* Many a horse is ruined by allowing the legs to go dirty. It takes only a few minutes to wash them clean and rub them dry. If the skin begins to crack it must not be left or it will become almost incurable. The skin must be kept clean and soft. Cut the hair off short and paint it over with chloride of zinc and water—thirty grains to one pint of water. Put this on once a day and rub with glycerine.

Horses having greedy appetites, rough coats and poor condition may be suspected of *Worms.* Such animals often pass long, round worms. Copperas or tobacco will clear the worms out of the stomach of a horse. A tablespoonful of copperas for two days and then stop for two. A handful of tobacco dried and made into powder and mixed with the grain. Give this for three days and then hold on for a few days. For worms in the rectum a syringe must be used. Salt and water is good ; carbolic acid diluted fifty times in water, or, what is better, thymo-cresol. This would undoubtedly be a good internal remedy for worms, diluted one to fifty parts of water. A tablespoonful of the thymo-cresol diluted with a quart of water would make a good dose as a worm exterminator.

Some horses, although having a good appetite, remain gaunt and thin from *Indigestion*. They should be given some strong purgative, like Barbadoes aloes, combined with powdered ginger, one-half ounce; Glauber's salts, one-half pound, dissolved in a quart of water. When the intestines have been thoroughly cleaned by this process, give daily the following powder: Sulphate of iron, three drachms; sulphate of soda, two ounces; nux vomica, ten grains; ginger, one-half ounce. This powder may be continued daily for a month. Give all the rock salt the animal will lick.

Spasmodic Colic begins suddenly. The horse stamps impatiently, looks backward, soon paws, and then rolls. After an interval of ease the pains return with increased severity. Give chloral hydrate, one ounce, in half a pint of water as a drench; or ether and laudanum, two ounces each, in linseed oil, half a pint; or sulphuric ether and alcohol, two ounces of each in eight ounces of water. If nothing else is handy, give of whisky half a pint in hot water. If not relieved in one hour repeat any of the doses prescribed. The body should be warmly clothed and sweating encouraged. Dip blankets in hot water containing a small quantity of turpentine and hold them in place under the body with dry blankets, or rub the abdomen with stimulants or mustard water. If cramp is due to irritation in the bowels, a cure is not complete until a physic of aloes, one ounce, or linseed oil, one pint, is given. Soapy or salt water aid the cure when used as an injection.

Wind Colic is caused by feeding after long fasting, or when the animal is exhausted by driving, or by new grain or hay, too much grain fed, or by sour or indigestible food.

The horse seems dull, paws, and the pains are continuous. The belly enlarges, and when struck in front of the haunches sounds like a drum. If not soon relieved, difficult breathing, sweating, staggering and death follow. Give alkalines to neutralize the gases formed. No simple remedy is better than common baking soda, two to four ounces. If this fails, give chloride of lime in half-ounce doses, or the same quantity of carbonate of ammonia dissolved and diluted with oil or milk until relieved. Chloral hydrate is particularly useful in both wind and spasmodic colic. Horsemen would be wise to keep it ready for emergencies. Physic should be given in flatulent colic, and turpentine, one to two ounces, with linseed oil, eight ounces, frequently, to stimulate the motion of the bowels. Colic should not be neglected nor the patient left until certain of cure or death.

For *Sore Shoulders* in horses, the best thing is to have properly fitting collars. If the surface galls under the collar wash with salt and water at night and with clear water in the morning, and protect the spot with a pad under the collar. If the skin breaks use a lotion of one drachm of carbolic acid to one quart of water twice a day, and relieve the horse from work for a day or two. It is cruel to work a horse with a raw sore shoulder.

Choking Distemper prevails at times in many parts of the country. It is sometimes called spinal meningitis or putrid sore throat. The animal often falls down paralyzed, cannot arise, and if left prostrate is almost sure to die. He must be got upon his feet, and if he cannot stand must be swung. A majority of cases are fatal. It is caused by some specific poison taken into the system with food or drink, mostly the former. Dirty mangers, rotting roots or meal, and mouldy hay, especially meadow hay, are usually the medium by which the disease is acquired. The moral is to have everything sweet and clean that the animal eats and drinks, and have no decayed matter in the entry or in any other part of the barn.

The peculiar movement of the abdomen and flank, point to *Heaves*, and a cough usually accompanies it. There is no cure for the established disease. Careful dieting will relieve the distress, but this will appear as bad as ever when the stomach is overloaded. The best quality of food lessens "heaves." Food that is too bulky and lacks nutriment, has much to do with the disease. Feed affected animals only a small quantity of hay once a day, and invariably water at least fifteen minutes before feeding, and never directly after meal. Work right after eating aggravates the symptoms. Carrots, potatoes or turnips, chopped or mixed with oats or corn are a good diet. What bulky food is given should be in the evening. Medical treatment is worth less than dieting. A predisposition to the disease may be inherited.

If *Dysentery* exists, place the horse in a dry, well-ventilated stable, rub the surface of the body frequently, and keep it and the legs warm with blankets and bandages. The food must be light and easy to digest, the water pure and in small quantities. Give first, castor oil one-half pint and laudanum two ounces. The strength must be kept up by milk punches, eggs, beef tea, oatmeal gruel, etc.

A GOOD PULLER.

Chapter VII.

AILMENTS AND REMEDIES—CONTINUED.

Glanders—Gorged Stomach — Lockjaw—Choking—Hooks
—Lice—Knuckling— Ring Bone—Spavin — Scratches—
Itching Skin—Overdriven Pace.

When cooled and rested,
Give me water and feed;
And I'll willingly serve you
In time of need.

Whenever a horse is seen to bleed or emit offensive matter from the nostrils, *Glanders* is suspected and treatment should not be attempted. It may be a dangerous case, which is fatal alike to man and beast. A veterinary surgeon should be called.

Gorged Stomach results when a horse has been fed after a long fast. The small stomach of a horse is so distended that it is unable to contract itself upon its contents, a motion which is necessary in digestion. The horse becomes stupid, slight colicky symptoms are observed, and he carries his head low and extended. As he grows worse he paws, becomes delirious, is covered with cold sweat, trembles, slobbers, staggers and drops dead. Treatment is difficult. A purgative of Barbadoes aloes, one ounce, should be given at once, followed by Cayenne pepper, one-half ounce, or Jamaica ginger, one-half ounce. If the bowels can be stimulated to act, they will in a measure relieve the stomach. For this purpose use turpentine, two ounces, and linseed oil, eight ounces.

Horses liable to *Staggers* and *Fits* should have harnesses that are carefully adjusted, and should not be pushed in hot weather.   No heavy feed should be given them at any time, oats and sweet hay or grass being the best.   Such animals should not be driven when it can be avoided.   When indications point to an attack, the horse should be stopped, his harness loosened, some cold water given him to drink and his face sponged at the same time.   Rye is a bad feed for sleepy staggers.

Lockjaw is caused by cuts, nail in the hoof, etc. Nothing is so common from wounds in the feet and from docking. The horse is unable to open his jaws to the fullest extent, and mastication is impossible.   Various muscles twitch, the head and tail are elevated and the nose protruded, and the anus is compressed.   The animal swallows with difficulty ; saliva flows from the mouth.   Of course, in this disease the necessity of calling in a skilled veterinary surgeon is indicated.

A horse which is frequently or occasionally overtaken with *Giddiness* or *Megrims* is dangerous to use. This trouble is hard to cure.   It indicates the need of moderate driving, especially in hot weather, and that a small amount of hay should be fed.

Horses that are *Choked* thrust out their heads, bend and stretch the neck, while there is a copious flow of saliva from the mouth.   In some cases there is distention of the gullet on the left side of the neck, if it have descended so far.   If it be in the upper part of the gullet a man accustomed to giving balls may be able to reach it with his hand. Obstructions that have got lower down may be moved upward gently from the outside.   Sometimes an obstruction is soft and may be crushed small enough for the animal to swallow it.   A mass of meal or other impacted food is sometimes removed by frequent drinks of water, and a drench of olive or cotton seed oil can do no harm. The plan of reaching a whip or heavy piece of rope down the gullet to push the substance into the stomach is risky, in the hands of one not accustomed to the anatomy of the horse.

Lampas is usually an imaginary trouble. Very rarely does the membrane directly beneath the upper front teeth congest and swell enough to interfere with feeding. When this trouble is feared there is no quicker nor surer cure than feeding a little corn in the ear. When biting off the kernels, the horse naturally compresses the membrane or forces it back. The burning of the lampas is cruel and unnecessary, and if the swelled parts are cut, the cut should not be deep, or danger will result.

There is a widespread delusion that *Hooks*, so called, is a disease affecting the horse's eye. A barbarous custom among cruel men is to forcibly destroy the membrane which keeps the eye free from foreign substances, but the cruelty does not accomplish the desired result, though it may injure or destroy the eye. The obstinacy of the membrane simply shows something to be wrong in the anatomy of the horse, just as the tongue will indicate to the observing physician when the stomach of his subject is out of order. To cut or disturb the hooks in the eyes is as absurd as to doctor the tongue instead of the stomach in the human case.

Remove *Lice* by rubbing the animal with a solution of sulphate of potassium, four ounces, and water, one gallon, or with strong tar water ; or dust with Persian insect powder ; or the skin may be sponged with benzine or quassia chip tea. Any of the applications must be repeated a week later to destroy the lice hatching in the interval. All blankets should be boiled, and the stalls painted with turpentine, and littered with fresh pine sawdust.

Knuckling, or cocked ankle, is a condition of the fetlock joint which resembles partial dislocation. The trouble is not considered unsoundness, but it predisposes to stumbling. Foals are quite subject to it, and no treatment is necessary, as the legs straighten up naturally in a few weeks. It is caused in horses by heavy and fast work, and is produced sometimes by a disease of the suspensory ligament, or of the flexor tendons. This should be relieved by proper shoeing. The toe must be shortened and the heels left high, or the shoe should be thin forward with thick heels or high calks.

A *Splint* may be rubbed off and the work aided by putting on a liniment, but few would persevere in the rubbing long enough to make a cure. A blister will do it.

If the *Fetlock* be *Sprained*, and the injury slight, bandage and apply cold water frequently. Where the lameness is intense, and the swelling and heat great, the leg should be kept in a constant stream of cold water. When the inflammation has been subdued the joint should be blistered.

Ring Bone is an osseous exudation or bony deposit at the crown of the hoof. When its presence is first detected the place should be severely blistered once or twice, or red iodide of mercury applied. If this fail, firing with the hot iron in the hands of a competent surgeon will be necessary.

If you have a suspicion of a *Spavin* coming on your horse, employ a good veterinary surgeon. Heroic treatment is the only thing in such cases. Judicious firing, strong blistering and perfect rest for at least six weeks or two months, and good nursing will, in most cases, arrest the disease and cure lameness. It is the result of too great exposure in draught or speed, or from slipping and kindred causes.

Scratches or grease is frequently proof of carelessness in clearing stables, and includes poor ventilation. The trouble may result from condition of the blood, from unwholesome fodder, or work in irritating mud or dust, especially of a limestone character. It has been brought on by using caustic soap on the legs, clipping the heels in winter time, by debilitating disease, etc. The first step in a cure is to remove the cause, and if there is much local heat, administer a laxative like a pound of Glauber's salts. Highly-fed animals should have their rations reduced, or replaced by bran mashes, flaxseed, fruits, roots, and other non-stimulating food. Bitter tonics are essential also, and may be continued six weeks to two months. If the skin is unbroken, bathe with water, one quart, in which sugar of lead, two drachms, is dissolved, or annoint with vaseline, one ounce, sugar of lead, one drachm, and carbolic acid, ten drops. To clip the hair from the horse's heels and poultice them with grated carrot, night and morning, is sometimes beneficial. Free exercise is important. Rub the heels dry and apply equal parts of glycerine and compound tincture of aloes.

The treatment for *Wind Galls* consists in pressure by means of bandages and by cold lotions. Blistering will remove them. *Capped Hocks* are reduced in the same manner.

There is no treatment that will surely avail in the cure of *String Halt*.

For *Itching Skin*, wash the skin thoroughly with carbolic soapsuds, and give the horse a half pound of Glauber's salts daily for a week. Do not feed him any grain but wheat, scalded bran and linseed meal, three quarts of the former and one quart of the latter, for two weeks. There will speedily come a change. Card him daily. Scald his oats and give him salt daily. Feed oats, bran and linseed after the two weeks and scald the whole mess. When horses are covered with bunches or lumps, their blood is out of order.

Give doses of Glauber's salts daily and hot bran mashes. Give salts a half pound daily. A gill of *raw* linseed oil every day will be good, mixed with the bran.

The horse which eats its own excrement does it for the acids it contains, which are voided in it and in the urine which it has absorbed. Give such a horse a *pinch* of copperas, bone dust, salt, ashes and saltpetre mixed in its meal once a day. A few days of pasturing is good.

Horses snort and wheeze because of an enlargement of the glands in the nostrils. A skilled veterinarian can remove the trouble by cutting it out. Doctoring will not cure snoring or wheezing horses. The air passages are stopped.

A twenty-year-old horse was not doing well. Upon examination his front teeth were found to be so long that his grinders were kept from coming together, and he could not masticate his food. His teeth were filed off, and the sharp points evened with a float, and he is now doing as well as any of the younger horses. Watch the teeth of the old horse.

An experienced horseman, if human, will not push his horse beyond his strength by *Overriding* or *Driving ;* still at times an indiscreet driver will bring an animal to the verge of extinction, when it is well to know what to do for him. The symptoms are plain in the audible breathing, staggering gait, exhausted appearance and heaving flank. The girts must be removed and the face turned toward the wind, the animal being protected from the sun meantime. The head must be left free and the limbs and body well rubbed. The movement of the ribs should not be hindered in any way. A few swallows of cold water may be allowed, and, in hot weather, the mouth, forehead and face may be sponged with it. When sufficiently revived the horse should be slowly led to a comfortable box-stall and heavily blanketed, woolen bandages being wound about the legs as well. If the horse has fallen he must not be allowed to lie until he voluntarily gets up, but must be propped up on his breast and not allowed to lie flat on his side.   Heat exhaustion is somewhat similar in symptom and demands similar treatment, with the addition of throwing cold water over the animal, particularly wetting the head, and causing a current of air to pass over him that evaporation may take place.

NEVER SICK A DAY IN HIS LIFE.

CHAPTER VIII.

DOCTORING.

Giving Medicine — Medicine Ball — Injections—Physic —
Condition Powders—Ending a Horse's Life.

Many inexperienced horsemen know nothing of how to
give a horse medicine. Some who can administer a drench
have never tried balling. Many get bitten who try, so it is
best to be careful. Hold the head high, reach the fingers into
the animal's mouth just back of the forward teeth where there
are no teeth, and no danger of being bitten, and grasp the
tongue, pull it out gently, and as you do so the horse will
open his mouth, allowing the tongue to loll between the
grinders. The medicine ball may then be safely pushed
down the animal's throat as far as the hand can be made to
reach, for the animal will not attempt to close his jaws while
his tongue is between them. Two persons, one to administer
the medicine, while the other is holding the tongue and
head, will accomplish the desired object more quickly. The
throat should be watched carefully, and the animal not be
allowed to lower his head until he is seen to swallow. The
tongue should be pushed back into his mouth as soon as the
ball is put well down the throat, as it will assist in the swal-
lowing process. Horse balls usually come wrapped in
tissue paper, and should not be unwrapped before administering, as it prevents bad taste in the mouth.

The giving of a drench is so easy and common as not to
need description. The medicine should be shaken well with

half a pint of water, and poured into a wide-mouthed heavy glass bottle that the horse cannot easily crush. Having secured the head and tongue as described in "administering a ball," turn up the bottle in the horse's mouth, holding the head so the contents will run down his throat. Remove the bottle after pouring in about four ounces. If he does not swallow at once, gently close the nostrils for a moment, or tickle the roof of his mouth with the finger nail. This will cause him to move the tongue and before he knows it he will have swallowed the mixture. If coughing occur or the bottle be crushed, lower the horse's head immediately.

Injections should be small in quantity when for absorption, and at a temperature of 90 to 100 degrees. They should be introduced only after the last bowel has been emptied by hand or by copious enemas. Clysters are given usually to aid the action of physics, and should be in sufficient quantity to cause the animal to eject them. Warm water, salt and water, or soap and water, one gallon or more at a time may be given every half hour. It is best that they be not discharged immediately. Liquids may be injected by means of a large syringe, or by a simple funnel made for the purpose of a two-quart pail or pan seven inches in diameter, to which a pipe sixteen inches long is soldered at right angles. This pipe is introduced into the rectum and must be made perfectly smooth and be oiled before using. Pour the liquid into the funnel rapidly after it is inserted, and the bowels will be drenched as quickly and effectively as by a more complicated arrangement, and in safety. Or a common funnel and rubber pipe will answer a better purpose. Besides those described, there are few or 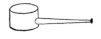 no other methods for administering doses that are necessary or safe enough for the novice to attempt.

An excellent physic ball for a horse is made of powdered Barbadoes aloes, seven drachms, powdered gentian, two drachms, and sufficient syrup to stick it into a hard ball. The ball should be three or four times as long as its diameter. When a horse has been physicked severely he should not have any hard exercise for several days, but should be walked a little every day and allowed to stand in the sun. Bran mashes should take the place of his regular ration for three feeds, water often, but sparingly, even if thirsty.

Condition powders for horses are not only expensive and undesirable, but frequently unsafe as well. Recent analyses of condition powders selling by the package at the rate of $1,000 per ton, have been found to contain linseed meal principally, with small quantities of camphor and other drugs, more or less harmful, in varying amounts, the mixture not costing the manufacturers over $28 to $30 per ton. As a natural tonic for the system, the safest and best condition powder permissible under all conditions is good food, perhaps placing linseed meal at the head of the list of grains. It imparts strength and tone to the system, nourishing the nerves as well as the muscles, acting like a gentle laxative upon the bowels, mellowing the hide, glossing the coat, and removing it betimes in the spring. No prescription is better than the following, as a rule: Dried sulphate of iron, two drachms, powdered gentian and powdered fenugreek, of each four drachms, all in one powder, to be put in the feed night and morning for three weeks.

There is danger in using many of the advertised tonics and condition powders which contain arsenic. These benefit animals at first, but not permanently.

How to poultice a horse's leg is often a problem, especially when the poultice must be kept at a point high up or arching. A bag is prepared a little larger than the leg, and with no bottom.   Around the lower edge a puckering string is run in to tie around the leg.   Next, cords two-thirds the length of the bag are made fast to the top of it, and then sewed to the bottom, so the lower third pouches below and outside of the puckering cord.   The top is held up by cords fastened to old harness, kept on the horse.   The poultice is poured in, a bountiful quantity being used.   Such a bandage will hold it in place without waste or failure unless the injury itch or pain severely.   Then the animal will use its teeth upon it, if allowed to reach it.

If animals must be killed, humanity requires that it be done in the quickest and least painful manner. For shooting a horse, place the pistol muzzle within a few inches of the head, and shoot at the place marked above by a dot, aiming toward the center of the head.   If it must be done by blows, blindfold, and with a heavy axe or hammer strike at the same spot as above.
Two vigorous, well directed blows should make death sure. Be careful not to shoot or strike too low.

If there is no other way to get rid of dead carcasses cover them with earth a few inches deep and burn them.   The earth will absorb a good part of the gases and when burning put on more.   When all burned, cover up well with earth and then mix the mass and sow it broadcast on any land and it will tell wonderfully.

Spare me up and spare me down,
But spare me not on level ground.

MARE MAXIMS.

John Tucker says:

Don't breed scrubs. It's wicked.

If we breed our colts in the autumn we reduce their cost, as the mare can do team work all summer.

The same mare to the same horse and all the neighbors doing the same thing will get the matches.

Mares bred at home, not traveled, are more sure. In many cases it would be better to take the mare to the stable of the sire before the time of heat and leave her a few days after service. Anyway, she should be walked all the way home.

The old mare should be kept breeding, for if you skip over a year she may not conceive again. Mares will breed usually till twenty, and often for years after.

We would not risk feeding rye to mares in foal, as the ergot which is so common in rye acts directly on the womb and uterus. Ergot is a poison.

If you have a colt arrive, don't feed the mare largely on hay for a week or two. Give her nourishing and more con-centrated foods. Her form will be better.

Pick out clean legs and a good temper, as well as perform-ance and pedigree, if you are buying a mare to breed.

Heavy mane and tail look pretty, but seldom are marks of a good horse.

Chapter IX.

MARE AND COLT.

Have an Aim in Breeding—Breeding Farm Horses—The Foal—Feeding the Colt—General Observations.

A good mare will pay the mortgage.

Keep the trotter notion out of your head. Trotters make mortgages.

FAMOUS IN THEIR DAY.

We should rear our own teams and then we can know of what they are made. When a man buys a horse he does not know how many hereditary spavins, ring bones, curbs or blind eyes, or how much heaves he is purchasing at a big price per pound.

Have an aim in breeding and try to breed all of the colts to a standard. They will then make pairs and sell for more. A whole town should unite in this and make a reputation for good horses and horses alike. Where this is done money will flow in like a steady stream.

Defects caused by accidents should not debar a good mare from being a breeder. Such as pin-hipped, or injuries caused by overwork or bad shoeing. Avoid a kicker, a puller or a balky mare.

Many a man owning a valuable road mare will not breed her because he dislikes to spoil her shape. But this trouble can be entirely prevented by care directly after foaling. The dam has a feeling of emptiness succeeding parturition, and will eat abnormally if not restrained. If this inclination is controlled for three or four days she will return to her normal form. Soothing, laxative and nutritious food must be administered and no stuffing done with hay.

The farmer should never fool with trotters unless he happens to have a genuine, full-bred trotting mare, and if he has such a one he should sell it. Paper trotters are no good, neither are those which make fast time around barroom stoves. Blood will tell with trotters, but it must be there. The last kind of horses for farmers to breed are the expected trotters.

What are you going to do? Are you going to breed farm horses? Then get a pony-built, solid mare and take her to the same kind of a horse, weighing about 1,200 pounds. You want a mare and horse with a good, strong walking gait and a square, steady trotting motion. Avoid the lungers, the high-steppers and the fast trotting action. Such horses will not settle down to the slow and steady gait required on the farm and for hauling loads, and they are not so strong. They will fret and fume and tear themselves all to pieces.

Going to such sires and using such dams to breed work horses
is cruelty to man and beast.   A horse is fitted for its business
just as much as a minister, a lawyer or a doctor.   And when
you get one out of its natural profession you make a mistake.
Such animals will do better to go single; but then they are
apt to be fretty.

   If the mare is difficult to get with foal or has never had a
colt, take her to the sire at the first heat in the spring.   Try
a young horse which has been exercised all winter.   If these
attempts fail turn her to pasture with a stud colt, and let her
run there a couple of months.

It is a mistake to work a mare all day and tire her out,
and then take her to the horse.   The best time is in the
morning when she is not exhausted.   Let there be full vigor,
and never force at the time of stinting.

A foal may come any time, but in the early spring is
best.   Autumn colts will do well if carefully wintered.   Colts
born in midsummer—fly-time—should be housed during the
day, and the mare fed green food.   These extra cares are
an objection to this time of breeding.   The surest time for
conception is the ninth day after foaling.

If a mare is inclined not to have much milk before foaling, feed her for six weeks ahead to produce milk.   Give
her clover hay; carrots, a peck a day in two feeds; wheat
middlings, six quarts and oats six quarts.   Rub her udder
several times a day and stretch it.

A mare carries her foal from eleven months to fourteen,
usually about eleven.

As mares vary so much in the period of gestation, the
only safe plan is to put your animal in a separate stable or
suitable box-stall at about ten months from service.

When a mare in foal gets all the clover hay she wants,
she has the best food she can have, and no grain is neces-

sary.   When she is fed mostly on straw, she requires bran
or oats to make up the elements required to keep up her
vitality and to make the colt strong.

Many persons think that a mare should rest from work for
several weeks before foaling.   It is not so.   If a brood
mare has been accustomed to farm work before she is with
foal, let her continue at such work, without forcing her, until
she is about ready to drop her colt.   Regular and moderate
exercise is as necessary to the health and comfort of horses
as it is of human beings, and in no way can brood mares
have it better than by being used in the manner to which
their muscles have been accustomed.   Of course, she should
rest a few days after the colt is born, on her account and the
colt's also.   Straining work is not good, but any kind of
light work will not injure.

To dry a mare up in her milk, feed her straw for a
few days, or a little hay, and rub soft soap on her udder.
Give her a reduced amount of water.   Milk the udder out
only partially each day.

Choose mares that are young, sound, roomy and of good
disposition.   They are better if larger than the horse, rather
than smaller.

The stallion must not have ring bone, navicular disease,
cataract, unsound feet or bad temper, however beautiful in
form he may be.

Impotency in stallions is caused more by want of exercise
than by any other cause.   Feeding fattening foods is also a
chief cause.   Moderate work is better than idleness.   Any

work which is not straining
is beneficial.

The paddock for a stal-
lion is drawn so as to show
the inside, which has a sloping fender four feet high to

prevent the horse from getting cast. It is a safe paddock. The door has its fender fastened to it, so that when shut the whole inside is protected alike. A scantling from the bottom to the side in the corners and middle keeps the fenders in place.

> *Good food, good water, these I need ;*
> *For kindness also do I plead ;*
> *Good grooming, too, will not be vain—*
> *' Tis health to me—to you great gain ;*
> *Daily, I beg, this care renew—*
> *This is your duty—this my due.*

If the foal be born in the fœtal membranes it must be liberated at once or it will suffocate. If the navel cord is not ruptured it may be tightly tied in two places near together and cut between the cordings, or it may be severed by scraping it with a dull knife about two inches from the navel.

Colts will bleed to death if the umbilical cord is severed too close to the body and too soon after the colt is born. Watch things to have the best luck.

If the dam will not lick it, then it must be carefully rubbed dry with hay and cloth and its hair left straight. It must also be kept warm. The first milk of the mare acts as a physic upon her offspring.

Be sure the little foal gets some suck. It is sure to do well if it should suck within a half hour after being born.

Don't be such a goose as to tie a mare that is due to foal. Give her a box-stall.

The sucking colt can be injured by his own mother's milk, if allowed to draw it while she is overheated from work or driving.

When the colt is born during the heat of summer it is not safe to leave the mare out in the sun with it until it is a few days old, as the colt will lie down and it may be killed by the heat.

A scouring foal should have careful treatment. Cover closely with a warm blanket with two surcingles, that it may keep his belly warm, and bandage the legs to arms and thighs. Drench with sixteen to twenty ounces of castor oil containing one-quarter ounce of laudanum. Give but little drink, and make it tepid. Feed rice boiled to a pulp in new milk, and one quart of new milk may be given daily. When the foal is stronger, give a few crushed oats and good old hay. A slight looseness of the bowels may cause no anxiety, as this is natural with young colts. If the little colt does not get milk enough, feed it milk and oatmeal made into a thin gruel.

The greatest trouble with little colts, when young, is constipation. This may be regulated by giving the mother sloppy food, such as scalded bran. If the foal is bound up, when born, give it an injection at once of starch, molasses and warm water. Repeat every half hour until relief comes. As he gets older, relieve constipation with linseed meal, potatoes or carrots.

A great many farmers who raise colts don't seem to know that it pays to feed colts well from the beginning, and to make them grow as fast as possible. They should not feed for spavins, ring bones, and other blemishes or defects in the limbs, and yet they do. Some men's colts are always unsound in their limbs, and the reason is they do not have food suitable to make a perfect development of the bones, tendons, tissues and muscles.

Do not imagine the colt is all right because it has all the hay it can eat. This is not wisdom. Give it less hay and two to four quarts of bran and oats mixed, according to its size. This kind of food will make strong bone and joints.

What is a colt good for without good joints? They are worth more than size or style. We can have both, but by all means have good joints, and to get them there must be phosphates in the feed, and the bran and oats contain these.

If the little colt is fed cow's milk, it should be boiled, as it will then digest it easier.

A DAISY FOR THE YOUNGSTERS.

If the weanlings are kept in the stable, give them plenty of bedding, so that there will be some spring under their feet. Sawdust is good. Colts kept on a dry, hard floor will get sore in their joints and may become curbed or throw out ring bones. Standing on manure is not good. If the floor is wet and slippery they are likely to slip, and in this way become blemished.

Don't leave the colts out in a cold rainstorm. Better let them go hungry for a little while than expose them in this way.

Looks go a great ways. The colt that is groomed clean, and is made gentle and handy, will sell for a good price; while the unkempt, wild and unbroken colt, will not sell at all.

If the colt carries his tail on one side, employ a skilled veterinary surgeon who will cut a cord on the opposite side, which will remedy the difficulty and add fifty dollars to the value of your horse.

If the colt's ankles seem a little tired and weak after driving, bathe them thoroughly with cold salt and water and wrap them in bandages, but do not bandage them tightly.

If a colt should turn out to be very excitable or nervous, the feed of oats should be cut down or stopped altogether.

TAKEN ON HIS FIRST BIRTHDAY.

Chapter X.

THE COLT'S EDUCATION.

It Should Begin Early—Some Methods—Gentleness Necessary — Tying Securely — Forming Good Habits — In General.

A colt should be really broken before it is ever put before any vehicle, and then there will be little trouble with it. To

hitch a wild and unmanageable colt to a wagon or a sleigh the first time is about as foolish a thing as can be done. It should be taught to do everything required of it except pulling at the collar, before it is ever made fast to anything, and then there is no danger of its getting frightened and learning any tricks. A promising colt may be ruined in a minute with such foolishness. A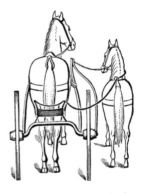
colt learns one thing at a time, and to attempt to crowd the whole horse education into it at once, and its first lesson, shows more jackass than horse sense. Go slow, be cool, try little and persevere, should be the horseman's motto.

The young colt cannot be trained too early. In fact, the sooner he is disciplined the more quickly he is subjugated, and with the least danger to himself and owner.

After halter breaking, which should be begun so young that he will never know liberty of head, he should at first be taught to lead, by being tied opposite his dam on short trips.

Very soon he should be gently accustomed to the harness and taught its harmlessness, and then broken to the bit. Next, a strong line should extend from the bit nearest the shaft and fastened firmly to it, and another line should run from the opposite bit through the turret ring and to the hand of the driver. Thus, the pair can be driven together, the youngster's gait being constantly influenced, and quite a little speed developed without having him draw or carry any weight, and while he feels the conditions are perfectly natural. The only difficulty to be encountered will be that the colt will get in the way of the wheel. This is easily avoided by attaching a small bent pole to the shaft at one end and at the other end to a piece of iron in the shape of a wrench, which must be firmly keyed to the nut of the wheel, on the side where the colt is driven.

As the colt grows older, he may be attached by traces to a light bar extending from the shafts, and allowed to feel the collar, and get accustomed to all the shake and rattle of road gear, of which the unbroken three-year-old is at first so much afraid. The youngster may be too small for any harness at first, but it is easy to get up a simple and strong one.

If home-made (which it may be without expense), nothing besides leather is so good as two small manilla ropes, side by side. After the little harness is completed, soak it in fine tar, and dry it thoroughly, and it will be almost indestructible and easily washed.

The first lesson the colt should learn is confidence in the master. Getting mad and saying cuss words will not give a colt confidence, but gentleness and a little sugar will.

No harsh word should ever be spoken in the hearing of a colt. Everything should be done to teach him that man is his friend. His education cannot begin too early. The longer it is postponed, the more difficult it becomes, and the more patience it demands.

Care should be had when a colt is first driven not to get it heated, or it will become more restive, and slouch around in the harness, and likely enough stop, or try to lie down and roll.

Never work about a colt rapidly, as if in a hurry; it only makes him nervous, and this causes him to lose presence of mind. Whipping is rarely better than coaxing and petting.

If the colt is stubborn about taking the bit, lead it into a stall and put a rope with a slipping noose around its neck ; then put the bit into its mouth, doing the work as gently as possible. The colt will very likely pull back and choke itself. After a moment's choking relieve it and try again. With a few such lessons the colt will hold its head down and give no more trouble.

After the colt has learned to be guided by the bit, he should be used in various ways for a week before he is driven. The first lesson will be to get him accustomed to the harness. He should not be frightened by it, but carefully taught what it is. He should smell of it, look it over and learn it will not harm him, during several hours if necessary. Previous to driving, the colt should be led an hour every day and taught to draw by the collar and whiffletree many things like a stick of timber, bush, stoneboat or other things of which he is likely to be afraid in the future. He should become accustomed from the first to robes, umbrellas, high loads, blanketed cattle, steam rollers, locomotives and whatever else of which he is likely to be afraid. He must be quietly but firmly led up to the object of his fear, being talked to kindly meanwhile.

Tying. During the first two or three years of his life in servitude he should never be fastened by anything smaller

than a half-inch manilla rope, which should be long enough
to permit secure tying. And he should never be fastened to
anything he may break off or move. If he becomes afraid
of that to which he is tied or learns he can break loose he
will always make trouble about standing, and the horse
which has once run away can be depended upon but little
afterwards.

Shying at objects is made worse by harshness. Keep a
sharp lookout and a tight rein. Whenever the colt shies,
stop him and let him look at the object of his fear. If the
colt manifests great fear of the cars, do not drive him attached
to the carriage as near as possible, and then compel him by
harshness to stand.

Do not hitch up a colt and give him a chance to kick.
Don't trust him until he has gotten accustomed to everything.
Give him the benefit of the doubt, and let him wear a sure
anti-kicking strap that will nip in the bud any tendency in
this damaging direction. As commonly applied, the kicking strap is a useless appendage, as many horsemen have
found out to their sorrow. To be sure of its controlling
power in every case, have it strapped to the crupper and kept
at the root of the tail. If it slip up or down it is likely to
be a menace to the driver's safety. This vice is exceedingly
difficult for a horse to forget, and few are ever broken of it.
A good horseman says that in training a colt disposed to
kick up put a wooden or iron martingale on him—that is, a
forked stick like a pitchfork ; tie the forks firmly to the bit
rings ; put a mortise in the other end for the girth to go
through. He cannot kick up worth a cent with that on.

Fast Walking. A horse that can walk fast is always a
source of pleasure, while a slow walker is an abomination.
While much comes by inheritance, education is much to be
credited for a good road gait. No animal so quickly forms

a habit as does a horse. Give him the chance to form the habit of fast walking. Don't tire him out on the start before you ask him to walk, and then expect him to walk rapidly. Give him a chance to show his ability at a walk when he comes fresh from the stable. If he feels good, so much the better; keep him down to a walk for the first few miles and let him form the habit of walking like a tornado. The natural inclination will be to walk fast, at times almost breaking into a trot. If this is continued day after day with care that the colt does not become tired, a prompt, or even very fast walk, will be as natural to that colt as eating.

Time and persistent care taking are necessary to educate a colt into a good and pleasant roadster, but once done the horse will have a higher market value than any not thus carefully trained. What has been said of walking is true of other gaits. When the pupil is started faster than a walk let it be a good stiff gait of eight to ten miles an hour. See that the colt does not blunder along or move carelessly. Let this gait be maintained until he has changed to a walk, and, whether the beast walk or trot, let it be a good road gait, as if he had some ambition, though the top of his speed may not be aimed at.

Many serious accidents would be avoided if every colt were taught to stop at the word. Be patient, and try to teach but one thing at a time, and educate him so that he will not be startled by things hitting him.

What shall be done for a colt inclined to bite? Be kind to it; but if it bites, chastise it on the spot.

It is very easy to spoil a colt if he is kept tied up in a stall without regular exercise. Don't do it.

The young horse not yet fully broken should have but one driver. A firm, quiet tone of voice and gentle manner are invaluable traits in a trainer, and however spirited a colt may be, he will control himself even when badly frightened, when he hears the reassuring voice of his driver.

Don't let the little colt follow his dam at work all day or on a long drive. The tender cartilages in his limbs are not able to bear constant use. He must be where he can lie down and be at rest two-thirds of the time. When the mare is taken away, first shut him up where he cannot in any way injure himself. A plain box-stall without undulations in the floor, without manger or ties of any kind is best. No young animal is more likely to get into mischief, and none is so easily damaged.

COLT MAXIMS.

JOHN TUCKER says:

Is the colt uneasy because a botfly is about ? Don't kill the colt; kill the fly.

Above all things, don't train a colt in a weak harness. Have everything strong and heavy, if it has to be made of inch rope.

It is a poor rule that won't work both ways. The colt should learn to back as pleasantly as he draws.

Feed the joints of the colts. How ? With oats and bran.

If the growing colt reaches up for its hay it will tend to make it higher headed.

No lesson of greater importance can be taught the colt than of standing still while one is entering or leaving the wagon.

Be very careful when turning out or calling up the colts not to get them in the habit of being hard to catch. A horse that comes when called is worth more money on the farm than a shy catcher. Always treat the colts to something they like when they come to you, and never by a quick act scare them away.

Each time you take the colt near the cars and coax him into gentleness you make him more valuable. Whipping and loud talk only make him worse for the next time. A horse that loses his head about the cars is of little worth.

Chapter XI.

THE FOOT.

Description—The Barefooted Horse—Some Ailments of the Foot; How Caused and Cured.

The foot is a delicate package covered with horn in varying thickness and hardness, making wall, sole and frog. Besides containing the foot bones (coffin, navicular and part of the small pastern bones), it holds the sensitive laminæ plantar cushion and the lateral cartilages. It is thus beautifully described by A. A. Holcombe, D. V. S.:

" The sole incloses the hoof on the ground surface, having a V-shaped opening at the rear for the frog. It is produced by the velvety tissue, a thin membrane covering the plantar cushion, and other soft tissues beneath the coffin bone. The horn of the sole differs from the horn of the wall, in that its tubes are not straight and it scales off in pieces. The frog is a triangular body divided by a deep fissure, and is attached to the sole by its borders. The horn of the frog is produced in the same manner as the sole, but it is soft, moist, elastic. It is the function of the frog to destroy shock and prevent slipping. The sensitive laminæ are thin plates of soft tissue covering the anterior surface of the coffin bone. They are present in great numbers, and by fitting into corresponding grooves on the inner surface of the wall the union of the soft and horny tissue is made complete. The plantar cushion is a thick pad of fibrous tissue behind and under the navicular and coffin bones and resting on the sole and frog. They receive the downward pressure of the column of bones and destroy shock.''

It is easy to understand from the above something of the delicate character of the horse's foot.

Ordinarily the horses may be kept at work without interruption, whether barefooted or not. There is not one per cent. of danger in this respect which is usually feared. If the barefooted horse actually becomes so tender as to limp, a condition of affairs which will rarely be seen except under the severest circumstances, the tenderness will only be temporary and in no way injure his value. If this stage should develop, thin, light toe-clips may be tacked on, or a piece of the best sole leather shaped to fit the foot and nailed to it the same as a shoe. When this is worn off the foot will have regained its natural toughness and none of the elasticity of the frog will have been destroyed meanwhile. Some horses with thin soles will require this protection for a short time, more, however, because of stepping upon small stones, etc., and causing temporary change of gait, than because the foot is worn down. Actual wearing is beneficial rather than otherwise, as it encourages nature to put forth an effort toward self-protection, which results in bigger, better feet, including a growth of that wonderful cushion, the frog. The leather shoe will require close watching, and the teamster should carry pincers to remove the nails at any time they project in a way threatening to scratch the horse.

Go slow about having the colt shod. If he has been allowed sufficient exercise his feet will be strong and tough, and you may go right on working and driving without shoes by standing in wet clay occasionally an hour or two. Should his hoofs become short and tender, have him shod with tips, which are very light, short, narrow shoes, only reaching back to where the last nail is usually driven, leaving the

heels without protection. The shoe to be countersunk into the
hoofs until on a level with the heels, never paring the frog,
heels or sole, and only putting in four nails, two on a side.
Now your colt can work and travel again, the frog taking
hold of the ground and preventing slipping. If he is required to do heavy pulling on rough, hard, frozen and icy
roads, we know of no better appliance than the customary
shoe with short, sharp toes and calks.

As soon as the necessity for the shoes is passed return to
the tips or no shoes at all. The horse accustomed to shoes
may have them removed when frost is gone. If hard and
brittle stand the hoofs in water two hours at a time and
poultice with cake meal at night. If the hoofs become too
short have on tips and exercise or work not too hard until
the hoofs regain their natural condition, when he will stand
the work, unless it be much upon the turnpike or he is flat-
footed, when we must use the old-style shoe until invention
brings something better. Use care and judgment in restor-
ing the feet to their natural condition, and you will be sur-
prised to find that many horses can do good service the year
around without shoes.

Lift up the horse's foot and see if the rim of the shoe is
inside of the shell of the hoof, and if it is start a boy with
that horse to the shoesmith, or take the chances of corns on
your horse.

An overgrowth of hoof and a consequent hardening of
the foot are fruitful sources of lameness. The elasticity of
the hoof is in itself a factor preventing lameness, dividing
up, as it does, the effects of concussion between the hoof
and the 500 sensitive laminæ that connect it to the foot
within the hoof-box.

Keep the feet pliable by soaking them occasionally during
the drouth of summer. A horse whose feet are too dry will

often flinch and limp on striking against or stepping upon
an obstruction, when he would not mind it in wet weather.
Don't oil the hoof. It does not take the place of water, and
filling the hoof cells keeps out moisture when it comes.
Soak in a tub, or by packing the feet with linseed meal
mush or wet moss. If a tub is not handy, stand the horse
on a thick blanket folded several times and soaked in water.
Moisten the walls by a loose bandage about each fetlock,
pouring on warm water frequently.   Many of the hoof oint-
ments, moreover, are positively injurious if regularly used to
any extent.   They are generally of a character to injure the
hoof, shutting up the pores in the horn, thus retarding or
preventing the natural and proper circulation in the hoof and
producing ruinous results.

When some horses lie down they strike the back part of
the fore leg with the calks of their shoes and bruise it. After
awhile a callous comes on and a sore.   The only way to
prevent it is to put a thick pad around the horse when standing in the stable, to keep the shoe from bruising the place.
Dress the sore with any sort of liniment, and grease it till
it is healed.

Puncture. It is dangerous for a horse to step on a nail, as
it is likely to result in lockjaw.   Have the blacksmith cut
out the puncture down to tender flesh, then fill the opening
with a five per cent. solution of carbolic acid and pack with
cotton to keep out dirt, and repeat daily, soaking the foot in
clean warm water before dressing.

Navicular Disease is indicated by a shrunken shoulder,
and a contracted foot that is placed several inches in advance
of the other while at rest.   This is an inflammation or ulceration of the pedal sesamoid at the point where the tendons
play over it.   The symptoms are often very obscure, according to the stage of the disease, and the lameness is attributed

to some difficulty in the shoulder. This, however, is a mistake. It is due to the wasting of the shoulder muscles from disease. The cause is usually fast work on hard roads or pavements, causing slight inflammation, which being unnoticed or neglected, increases and ends in ulceration. The best treatment is to remove the shoe, pare down the hoofwall and round the edge to prevent splitting, then fire deeply in points around and above the coronet, follow up with one or more blisters of red iodide of mercury, one part, lard, three parts, and when the effects pass off, turn out the animal to pasture for six weeks. It is always best to consult, in this disease, a competent veterinary surgeon.

Corns originate in simple bruises. There is later an increased production of hoof, and the formation of a horny tumor which presses on the quick. If of recent formation apply a bar shoe and rasp down the bearing surface of the afflicted heel and avoid pressure. Soak the feet. A horny tumor must be pared to the quick and packed with tar. Shoe with a bar shoe and place a leather sole between it and the hoof. If the corn be further advanced the foot should be soaked in a bucket of hot water for an hour, and then poulticed. Any matter that has formed should be liberated, and if grit or dirt have got into the heel this should be cleaned out. Poultices should be kept upon the wound until it is healed and free from soreness. If the cause is so serious that matter has burst out at the top of the heel a veterinary surgeon only is competent to manage it.

Thrush is a disease which shows an excessive secretion of unhealthy matter in the frog, and is detected by its vile odor. A common cause is foul stables. The cure consists in cleanliness and the removal of the cause. The diseased and ragged portions of the frog should be pared and scraped and the foot poulticed for a day or two with oil meal and water, to which may be added a few drops of carbolic acid, or some powdered charcoal. The dressing should be changed daily, and, after every vestige of decayed substance is removed, the cleft of the frog and grooves on its edges should be cleaned and packed with oakum, held in place by leather nailed on with the shoe. Before packing cover the place with a good coat of sulphate of zinc, pressing well in. Horses especially liable to thrush may need to be protected in the stable by the use of boots. Sometimes other diseases combine with thrush, making a cure seem impossible.

To determine lameness in a horse offered for sale lead the animal onto a hard road and examine him from various positions, from before and behind, and from each side, to locate the lameness. The head bobs to that side of the body which is all right. If the lameness is in the left fore leg, the head drops to the right. In posterior lameness the weight of the body drops on the sound leg. That is, when the dropping of the hip or nod of the head occur on the right side of the body at the time the feet of that side strike the ground, the horse is lame on the left side. If the motions are to the near side when these feet strike the ground, the lameness is on the off side. The foot is more frequently the seat of lameness than any other part.

A slow trot is the best gait to determine lameness. He will show it more, and he should be trotted when first taken from the stable. Watch him coming out of the stable— some lamenesses are over after the first few steps. Some forms of lameness are only noticeable after a hard day's work or a hard drive. Never buy a horse until you see how he stands a hard day's work.

HORSE MAXIMS.

JOHN TUCKER says :

The way to lift the mortgage is to hitch two good breeding mares to it and bid them go.

The difference between a good horseshoer and a poor one: the one is a thinker, the other a tinker.

A clean stable is like a clean heart. It means better things.

Cast-iron rules will not do in horse management any more than in the family.

What is a horse good for without sound feet?

Some horsemen will lie, and about horses, too. It is mean, but it is so.

It's poor policy to be mooning round in the barn with a lantern.

Nobody is more fully humbugged than a farmer who swallows the pedigree of a mongrel stallion.

Bragging does not make a good horse.

The frog in a horse's foot is a buffet against lameness. Don't let the smith cut it. Let it be as large and as low as possible.

Light shoes are better than heavy ones for most horses. Calks are often added when they are not needed. Don't use them if the horse can do without them.

SHOEING.

Proper Treatment of the Feet in Shoeing—Mistakes Pointed
Out—Fitting the Shoe to the Foot—Contracted Feet—
Interfering and Striking—Frequent Shoeing Necessary.

Proper treatment of the foot is one of the principal requisites
in the care of horses. Ignorant blacksmiths damage more
horses than they benefit by the close
paring of the hoof at heel and sole,
and rasping of the walls. "Take
care of the shuck and the middle
will take care of itself." This
statement, made recently by one
of the best shoers I have ever
known, is the terse expression of
a great truth. It is his custom to put on the shoes cold,
after carefully fitting them to the hoof, which is rasped level
or pared as little as possible. He does not "clean up the
frog," "open the heels," rasp off the walls, thin the sole,
nor in any way disturb himself to circumvent nature's efforts
to protect that sensitive and beautiful creation—the horse's
foot—so wonderfully hung, adjusted and boxed.

The horse with contracted heels! what a bugbear he is,
and how the average bungler loves to get hold of him and
display his wisdom and ability (?). Contracted feet are produced by artificial conditions and faulty shoeing. The great

majority of horses thus afflicted, if allowed to go bare for a year or more, would have the defect remedied by that greatest of veterinarians—nature. The time to pull off the shoes and be sure the hoofs will not break up at the edges and allow the feet to become tender, is in the spring, as soon as the frost begins to come out of the ground.

Animals that have never been brought to the forge have feet well fitted by nature for hard usage, which are in themselves proof of man's folly in blindly following customs.

Where shoeing is a positive necessity, preparation of the hoof is of great importance. Closely observe the unshod foot when it comes to the ground. Every part of its surface sustains a portion of the weight and wear. The frog, which appears to recede from the level of the foot when held in the hand, settles down so that it also bears upon the earth. When we put on the shoe, the weight is seen to be suspended in the foot, especially when calks are allowed. The frog is merely pushed down. The sole, frequently pared out by the merciless smith, has no opportunity for usefulness, and the wall of the hoof, besides being forced to drag along the iron thus nailed to it, sustains upon its edge the entire weight of the animal, besides bearing the friction within.

When shoeing the colt for the first time, no preparation is required for a shoe further than slightly leveling with the rasp the ground surface of the wall. Horses constantly shod will be found to have a crust of horn near the toe. Wear at that point is prevented by the immovable shoe, which, at the heels, always has slight play, because not nailed, and the growth is retarded or worn down. The fact that an iron casing does not permit a normal wearing of the foot's surface, forces the horse to submit to this damaging condition of affairs, unless he is handled at all times with intelligence. For when the foot has got out of the proper level, a serious danger is imminent. Increase of horn at the toe throws the pastern into an oblique position, and undue weight upon the tendons and ligaments at the back of the foot strains them.

Heels that are too high throw improper violence upon the bones and joints of the extremities, much as would be the case in man were he forced to wear a high-heeled boot a little too short at the toe. But little danger of this kind may be anticipated in the barefooted horse.

The inexperienced horse owner forced to submit to the work of an incompetent farrier may secure sufficient accuracy of level by insisting that the surface of the wall or outer crust of horn be brought to a level with the firm, unpared sole. The sole requires no reduction whatever, and owners of horses who permit it to be gouged and carved are submitting themselves as well as their property to an injury which, in some cases, will be forever without remedy. Nature provides in her own way for any excess of growth of frog and sole. Those who thin the sole with the avowed purpose of giving it greater elasticity, overlook the fact that they are removing its natural defense against injury and disease, a defense which no substitute can make good.

Having been prepared, preparation of the shoe is next in order, and it should be made to conform to the foot. Whoever is not sufficient master of the hammer to fit the iron to the foot instead of burning the foot into the shape of the iron, should not be permitted to handle horses' feet. The best of nails should be used, and three nails well set on a side are usually as good as four. The use of thin plates during eight or ten months of the year is preferable to thick shoes with heavy calks, except upon the feet of horses forced to travel slippery pavements and haul great loads.

Another fault is fitting the foot to the shoe, frequently using a shoe that is too small and rasping down the foot to fit it. This is a diabolical practice, fatal to the last degree to the life of the foot. The rasp should have no place in a farrier's kit, unless it be for leveling the walls. The weight of the horse should be borne upon the walls, whose edges should rest upon the shoe. If these walls be rasped away, and the weight thrown upon the sole, and the outer covering of the foot destroyed so it will dry up and soon become incapable of holding the nails, what can be expected of the foot?

An excellent plan for helping horses with contracted feet is followed by a New England farrier with most beneficial results. It is to level the upper surface of the shoe at the heel before attaching it to the foot, the inner circle to be one-sixteenth to one-fourth of an inch higher than the outer circle. It will be seen that the walls of the foot rest thus upon a surface which tends to spread them constantly. As a result of this continued relaxed condition at the heel, the frog is encouraged to grow, the bars to develop, and in a few months the heel is seen to be changing its condition materially. His unalterable rule is, "Never use the knife to open the heel."

Horses compelled to wear shoes should have them reset as often as every three to four weeks, not alone for the comfort of the horse, but that his feet and general constitution may remain uninjured. Insist upon small nails being used, and as few of these as possible. The holes for the nails should not be made too near the edge of the shoe. If punched further from the edge they take thicker and lower hold of the walls of the hoof, and do not need to be driven so high as to approach the sensitive part of the foot. With a perfectly level bearing, three nails on either side will hold the shoe firmly. With uneven fitting, however, the shoe

OUR TOM.

soon works loose. When the shoe has been fitted and the
nails clinched, insist that rasping, painting or oiling the foot
to improve its appearance or make a neat job be left un-
done. In its natural state the entire hoof is kept covered by a
secretion which cannot be improved upon by man, and which
preserves the moisture of the foot. To destroy this by mixing
with it some foreign compound, or to cut off the minute tubes
which constitute the shell of the foot, is the worst of folly.

Interfering may be prevented at times by proper shoeing.
The outside of the heel and quarter of the foot on the injured leg should be lowered slightly to change the relative
position of the fetlock joint, thus carrying it in such a position that its mate may pass without striking it. A very
slight change will produce this result frequently. The
offending foot should be shod so that the shoe, and especially
the responsible point, is well under the hoof, and the shoe
should be reset every three or four weeks. Frequent wetting of the injured parts with cold water or salt and water
will remove the soreness and swelling unless the part is
badly calloused. A Spanish fly blister may then be necessary to reduce the leg to its natural condition, and may need
to be repeated in two or three weeks.

When a horse is in the habit of forging or striking his
hind feet against his fore ones, careful attention should be
given to the shoeing. It is due to quick action behind and
slow action in front. Shorten the toes of the fore feet and
put on light, nicely fitted and turned up shoes. Do the
same with the hind feet, but put on shoes somewhat heavier
than the fore ones. By this arrangement the horse will pick
up his fore feet quicker and the hind feet slower, thus ac-
complishing just what is wanted. If a quarter of a second
of time is thereby gained the fore foot will be clear out of
the way of the hind foot.

MAXIMS.

Most horses when tethered by a rope will injure themselves by sawing the rope against the groove above the hoof behind. To remedy this trouble, tie in a piece four feet long of stout canvas, making a soft roll in place of the rope.

If you spoil your colt—what about the horse?

If you caress your horse it will make it feel as happy as a woman experiencing the same sensation.

You do not gain the confidence of your horse by whipping him. More flesh can be whipped off a horse in one day than can be fed on in a week.

Rear your own horses. It will not pay to sell farm products at a cent a pound, and pay for horses with this money at fifteen or twenty cents a pound.

The scrub horse has a mission.   He is needed by men who think it is necessary to jerk on the lines every time they want to turn, and kick the horse when they want him to stand over.

Unsoundness and carelessness are twins.

Animals are such agreeable friends—they ask no questions, pass no criticisms.

Morally, the horse is better than any human being that ever lived.

Screens at the stable doors and windows save bushels of feed.

SOUND AND STRONG ALL THROUGH.

Chapter XIII.

A WORD FROM HARRIET.

Making the Horse Happy—A Cheerful Animal the Most Useful—Importance of Gentleness—The Horse's Good Qualities Pointed Out—The Docked Horse.

> *Of food and drink give me the best,*
> *From brutal treatment keep me free ;*
> *Give me when tired a little rest,*
> *And see how useful I can be.*

People ought to try to make their horses happy. A happy, cheerful horse will do more work and live longer, and thus be more profitable to its owner, than one whose temper is kept constantly ruffled, whose disposition is soured by ill-usage, and whose peace of mind is often disturbed by the crack of the whip, the hoarse voice of the driver, the strain of overwork, the discomfort of a hard bed, or the pangs of hunger and thirst. If one would have a good, willing and useful horse, let him treat  him so that he will be cheerful and happy.

There are many ways by which this result can be brought about. Gentle treatment is, of course, one of the most

effective. Never strike a horse in anger; never growl a
him, never jerk the bridle nor lines, so as to hurt his mouth;
never whip him, at least never severely whip him, and be
sure that you do not keep him in constant terror or expectancy
of a blow from the whip. How can a horse possess a cheerful mind if he be always on the lookout for a cut across the
back, over the sides or around the legs ! Indeed, he will
waste a vast amount of energy and nervous force every day
if kept in a state of suspense, occasioned by a free and reck-
less use of the lash. If any one doubts it, let him try such
treatment upon himself.

A horse ought to be talked to a good deal. He under-
stands what is said to him very well. An intelligent horse

knows more than a stupid, uncultured
man. He is a good deal better company.
He is cleaner, as a rule, and gives no
countenance to vulgarity or profanity. He
is more self-respecting. He is less given
to bad habits. He could not be induced
to chew nor smoke tobacco nor drink beer.

UNHAPPY HORSE.

Whatever he does he does frankly, with a
clear conscience ; yet how often his master, who rates himself his superior, will violate his conscience and do things
he knows are wrong.

A horse is moderate in the indulgence of his appetites.
When he gets enough to drink he stops drinking ; when he
eats enough he quits eating. He is not a glutton. He is not
quarrelsome unless made so by bad usage. He harbors no
animosity. He is at peace with all the world. He is gentle;
he is forgiving; he is faithful when other friends fail. He is
contented ; the vain ambitions of the world, its discontent
and its strivings after the forbidden or the unattainable, are
never his. Therefore, though often rated by the unthinking

as inferior to man, yet he is in many respects vastly superior to the cross-grained, profane, brutal, vulgar and ignorant men into whose ownership he oftentimes falls.

The stalls should be cleaned out every morning (and evening also if occupied through the day), and a nice, soft, clean bed made for the animal to rest upon. Many horses are injured in their feet and legs by having to stand upon a great pile of manure, from which the ammonia arises, for weeks and months. The ammonia is also injurious to the eyes, to say nothing of the harness.

No colt will acquire bad habits of any kind if brought up right. If a fault be discovered, as it should be, in the beginning, it can easily be corrected. Overlooked and allowed to run on for a time, it is then hard to eradicate. The owner of a balky horse, for instance, has only himself to blame. Gentle treatment, kind words, an apple, a wisp of hay and a little patience, will move any but an old and confirmed balker. Those who happen to own one of the latter will often find a small bottle of ether effective in changing the current of the horse's mind and inducing him to draw the load. Only in rare cases has it ever failed.

The women folks should become interested in the welfare of the horse. Go often to the stable and talk to them and pet them. Pat them on the nose, give them the apple skins, and occasionally a fair, sound apple or potato. They will soon become acquainted with you and learn to listen for your footsteps and to love you. Possibly they may develop as much real affection towards you as you can find elsewhere about the premises; if so this is a clear gain. If you have courage go into the stall with them; curry them, bridle or harness them when necessary; teach them to serve you, which, if you are kind to them, they will be glad to do.

He was a beautiful horse in his youth. His long tail added much to his beauty, and was a sure defense against tormenting flies. A rich man in the city bought him to match another horse, and the two were attached to the family carriage.

The tail was cut off, because, strangely enough, the bobtail, cut square, was more pleasing to the owner than the tail given by nature. That was the reason why the tail was docked, but the owner excused the docking by saying that the horse would hold the rein under the tail and thus imperil the lives of those who rode.

The horse did not at first miss his tail brush, for he was a rich man's horse and wore a net in summer; he was carefully groomed and kept in good condition. But occasionally his owner drove the horse to his box buggy, and, as he was a hard driver, he was overdriven, spoiled, and of course sold.

The horse then came into the possession of a grocer who had some compassion and provided a net to keep off the flies. But at length the horse becomes too slow for the grocer, and then began the downward road that ends always in misery and torture.

Last summer this horse was seen attached to a fruit hawker's dilapidated wagon. It was a hot day, and the horse was standing in front of a fruit store while the owner was within buying his stock in trade. A more pitiable horsesight was never seen. The flies swarmed around him and drove him nearly frantic; he twisted, kicked, turned and bit himself till the blood had started. There was a fresh bruise on one hip on which the flies settled, the short hair of the tail was not long enough to reach this, and he was robbed of all defense.

The horse was little more than skin and bone, but he may have had food enough. His condition might be due to this continual worry and fighting of flies. If the man who caused the tail to be docked could have seen the horse in his present condition he would have regretted the part he took in it, if he had any feeling of compassion. Let every man remember who cuts off a horse's tail, cuts off not only the hair, but also the stump of the tail, that another stump will not grow in its place, and that the horse will be practically tailless the rest of his life. Horses were given tails because they need them, and it ought to be a crime, punishable by law, to mutilate a horse at the command of a soulless god-fashion.

TRY THIS, AND SEE HOW YOU LIKE IT.

COLT PHILOSOPHY.

HARRIET BIGGLE says:

A poor halter will often spoil a colt.

The time to train a colt is all along.

Give the young horses sunshine. They need it as much as they do pure air and exercise.

Make the little foal gentle ; sugar will do it, and kind words.

The teased colt often makes the vicious horse.

Teach the colt one thing at a time. When he has learned something don't let him forget it. Make him go over it again and again. In days following repeat it.

Make friends right off with the colts. Have some apples or something in your pocket for them, and they will soon come to feel that you are a friend. A horse loves a friend and hates an enemy.

Don't call a colt by a name that is too much like "whoa" or "get up." "Joe," for instance, is hard for him to distinguish from the order to stop. If you call him "Jacob" he will always think you are ordering an advance.

In these days of bicycles, accustom the colts early to their sudden or slow approach.

Chapter XIV.

AGE OF A HORSE.

How to Tell the Age of a Horse by His Teeth--The Age in Verse.

A horse's age is determined accurately only by referring to his teeth. Authorities differ somewhat as to the exact

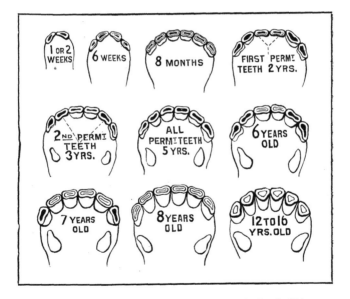

condition of the teeth at a stated age, and indeed all horses have not teeth of identical size and shape at a similar age.

But all agree that as the teeth come in, and later, as they wear down, definite appearances are presented, furnishing data that is fairly reliable for denoting the age of horses between birth and twelve years old, and less distinct proof for every added year. The accompanying jingles will prove a fair guide if carefully read and followed. The following, gleaned from the best authorities, is plainer, however, and carries the age table beyond the usual limit set, twelve years: Soon after birth two central nippers show. When a year old the colt has cut his twelve front teeth and sixteen grinders. When two years old, the mark on the grinding surface of the nippers (the two central teeth in the set of six), is much worn out and is hardly perceptible; it is not so faint in the middle teeth (teeth next the nippers), and the corner teeth are flat and show the mark clearly. During the third year the second set of teeth begins to show. Between three and three and one-half years the "baby" teeth or first nippers fall out and are replaced by permanent ones, giving the basis for after judgment as to the animal's age. The teeth are continually worn away, the length is decreasing, sometimes regularly and sometimes not, so that in old age the tooth once two and one-half to three inches long is scarcely half an inch long, unless the teeth slant forward too much, when they fail to get the wear which should occur, and they become very long. At four years the nippers begin to lose their sharp edge and have grown noticeably, the adjoining or "middle" teeth have also grown, but not fully, and are still sharp, with the deep mark plain. The corner teeth remain until the age is four and one-half years. After five years the age is learned by the shape and appearance of the teeth.

Now, the lower jaw shows nippers worn so the marking in the center is almost obliterated, middle teeth with the outer edge only worn, and corner teeth grown to an even height, but not worn much, and hooks grown, but not worn. At six, the nippers on the lower jaw are worn even and the middle teeth have still a cavity. At seven, the same jaw shows that the middle teeth have become even, and both edges of corner teeth rub, but still retain a slight cavity. At eight, a mere trace of the mark is visible in the lower corner teeth. At nine, the upper nippers have almost lost their mark, the middle ones show a faint mark, and the corner teeth have a deeper mark than the middle ones. At nine, also, the upper corner teeth begin to show a curve in the surface. This curve gradually deepens as age increases. At ten, the mark in the middle upper teeth has changed from oblong to nearly circular, and at eleven, the same change is noticed in the corner teeth. At twelve, the lower nippers have become nearly round, while they were broad in youth ; the middle teeth become so at thirteen, and the corner ones at fourteen. At fifteen, the upper nippers are rounded ; the middle teeth follow suit at sixteen, and the corner teeth at seventeen. When eighteen, the lower nippers appear three-cornered ; at nineteen, the middle ones, and at twenty, the corner teeth get into style. At twenty-one, the upper nippers get the three-corner shape ; at twenty-two, the middle, and at twenty-three the corner teeth do likewise. If the teeth project unnaturally, and are very long, it is more difficult to judge of the age, as they have not worn down as they grew out, hence the markings deceive. Such horses may be suspected, also, of not properly masticating their food. This is a great defect, inasmuch as the same amount of food will do them less good, and encourages physical defects of serious nature, as time elapses. Old horses and those with weak powers of assimilation are expensive property. This is a fault chargeable to young and immature horses (horses less than five years old), and it renders them unfit for hard driving or work of protracted and severe character.

THE AGE IN VERSE.

Two middle " nippers " you behold
Before the colt is two weeks old ;
Before eight weeks two more will come ;
Eight months, the " corners " cut the gum.

The outside grooves will disappear
From middle two in just one year ;
In two years, from the second pair ;
In three, the corners, too, are bare.

At two, the middle " nippers " drop ;
At three, the second pair can't stop ;
When four years old the third pair goes ;
At five, a full new set he shows.

The deep black spots will pass from view,
At six years, from the middle two ;
The second pair at seven years ;
At eight, the spot each " corner " clears.

From middle " nippers," upper jaw,
At nine the black spots will withdraw ;
The second pair at ten are white ;
Eleven finds the " corners " light.

As time goes on the horsemen know
The oval teeth three-sided grow ;
They longer get, project before
Till twenty, when we know no more.

CHAPTER XV

ABOUT STABLES.

However expensive a barn may be it can never be suitable for horses if bad odors prevail, as is the case in very many stables, nor where dampness holds sway. Horses are placed with their faces to high stone walls very often, with no board lining and air space between to carry off the moist air. These walls are wet in summer by condensing the humidity

GENERAL WASHINGTON'S STABLE AT MOUNT VERNON.

in the warm air, and bristle with frost in winter from the same cause. Avoid them, and keep horses out of basement stables if possible. Indigestion, influenza and rheumatism are directly traceable to such environments. Proper construction, ventilation and absorbents make a stable that is sweet for horses and safe for men.

Wherever possible let the stable face the south, and put the stalls on the sunny side of the building. A well known reformer once said: "Light is one of the best preventives of crime," so also sunlight is one of the best preventives of sickness. No animal can do well living in the dark. Darkness or only dim light injures, and is the cause of much difficulty with driving horses. The sun is a direct aid to digestion. Bad digestion means weak nerves, a bad coat and a stamina generally impaired.

The stable should be a solid superstructure upon an honest foundation. Crevices in the covering, floors and foundation may be the cause of colds, catarrhs and stiffness, besides making an easy harboring place for rats.

Make the ceiling of the first floor not less than eight feet high. Any horse will then be safe in throwing up his head.

The doors which the horse uses should be wide and high, and divided in the middle, so the upper part may be left open if desired. They should be at least four feet wide and seven feet high, so that he may go in and out with ease, and run no chance of knocking himself. Sometimes a horse will hesitate when entering a doorway, and then suddenly rush in, showing plainly that he is afraid to go through, having hurt himself while once doing so. Have plenty of windows and at the back or side of the horse rather than directly in front. They should be capable of being opened.

Opinions vary as to the width of the stalls, some say four feet, some six feet, but five feet will be found to be a good width. If not boarded up all the way to the ceiling they should be high enough so the horse cannot see over nor quarrel with a mate. Four feet high at the back and seven feet high at the end towards the manger will be about right. They should be at least nine feet long for the average-sized horse. Make the divisions of two thicknesses of two-inch plank, breaking joints. Loose box-stalls should be not less than ten feet square.

No stable should be fitted with stalls so close to the siding that it is troublesome to back out horses. Such close quarters are hard to clean properly and are always unpleasant for handling horses, while the room saved is trifling. Fourteen

feet is the least that should be given from the manger to the
wall at the back. Fifteen or sixteen feet would be still better.

Have the feed-bins and watering-troughs arranged so that
they will be handy and save steps. It will pay to line the
bins with tin to keep out the rats and mice.

If you cannot afford to cement the stable floor fill it in
with clay, and ram it hard and smooth. Here is how to lay

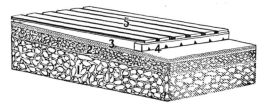

a cement floor—and have one by all means if you can. Dig
out the earth eighteen inches deep and fill in with the stones
to within six inches of the surface where the horse's feet
would be. Next ram down hard three inches of concrete
made of cement one part (Portland cement preferred), clean
sharp sand three parts, and screened gravel six parts. Wet
the gravel well and mix in the sand and cement thoroughly.
The mass must be sprinkled until it will retain any shape it
is pressed into. The surface coat is an inch thick, put on
before the first coat of concrete sets. It is made of three
parts sharp sand and one part cement. This is spread
smoothly, and must not be disturbed till the entire floor is
set hard like a block of granite. To induce it to dry slowly,
and so prevent cracking, it may be covered with a thin layer
of straw and sprinkled occasionally. If the hardening process takes two or three weeks, so much the better. The
whole surface must slope gently from the manger, say at the
rate of one inch to three feet. This will carry the urine
back so the horse will not get soiled nor be otherwise injured

by it—as, for instance, the injury to his eyes from the ammonia it often generates.

But the horse must not stand on this concrete else his feet will spoil it as he stamps at flies. A plank rack must cover it for a stamping surface. This is made of two-inch stuff, sawed four inches wide and laid three-quarters-of-an-inch apart on cleats. The rear cleat should be enough thicker than the front one to level up the floor. A level floor is necessary for the health of the horse's feet. Filth will collect between the slats of the floor, and must be cleaned out daily by the use of an iron or hook as thick as the spaces between the planks. The square and spirit level will be needed to make the floor a good one. It will save bedding and run off the urine into the manure vault or sewer. A bare cobble floor is not a satisfactory one for the horse, because so rough, hard and uneven; for the owner, because so hard on the horse's feet and so difficult to keep clean. In the engraving showing the stone and cement floor: 1 represents the space filled with cobbles; 2, the grouting of gravel and cement; 3, the inch of fine surface; 4, the thick rear cleat; 5, plank slats for the horse's feet. The foundation is placed thus deeply to avoid the action of frost.

Mangers should be made of the best seasoned oak, and so tightly that they will hold water. An inch auger-hole with a cork at its lowest point should permit water to be drained off in case of accidental spilling of a pail there. Mangers for horses inclined to gnaw should be protected upon the edges by sheet iron or wire net held in place by nails or staples. But this protection is as objectionable as iron mangers during freezing weather, as it freezes to the tongue and lips of the horse, skinning them. A broad surface like the bottom of the entire manger is better to feed grain in for most horses than a deep, narrow feed-box, as it prevents gorging and bolting of the food too quickly eaten. Induce horses to eat slowly for best returns from food. For a good grain-chute see the chapter on Feeding and Watering.

It is a poor plan to have the rack for hay up over the feeding manger as shown in the accompanying illustration. In this way the dust and dirt in the hay or fodder falls through the slats down into the feeding-trough. Then too the horse has to reach up, as if  he were a giraffe—an entirely unnatural position for him. When feeding naturally he has his head to the ground.

If the manger is divided into two parts, one for the grain and another for the hay, have the latter extend to within a foot of the ground and the bottom closed by slats six inches apart. The dust and dirt will fall through and can be cleaned away, with the bedding, without trouble.

If the hay is thrown down a chute into the entry, and then forked into the manger, never use anything but a fork with wooden prongs like that shown in the illustration.

The illustration represents a sensible arrangement in the stall for feeding hay. It is thrown into the chute from the mow above, and the horse pulls it out at the bottom where there are iron bars. He will usually pull out only what he eats. Make the chute gradually larger at the bottom than at the top, so that the hay will not lodge in it.

Given a good building, it must be so ventilated that while fresh air is kept abundant no drafts are permitted. Ventilators that reach to within twelve inches of the floor and extend through the roof will regulate this.

The accompanying illustration shows a convenient and easily made ventilator for barn or stable. It is a square box reaching from near the floor up and out through the roof. The bottom is open, but closes with a slide. Near the ceiling is a hinged door controlled by a cord, as shown. In warm weather this upper door can be opened to let out the heated air, which always rises. In cold weather this door can be closed, and the slide at the bottom opened to remove the foul gases that, from their greater weight than air, sink to the floor. The draft up through this ventilator will remove them.

Too often the chutes which bring down hay and oats are the only ventilation in a stable. They may be a source of much discomfort if not danger to the horse. Such chutes should be fitted with cross boards for sliding in, to close them tightly at top or bottom to stop air currents.

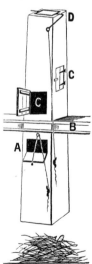

Hay or straw chutes may well serve as ventilators if they be closed always, where the hay is put in directly after using, and if they are carried up to the roof. A ventilator so arranged is here illustrated. The bottom should be two feet from the entry floor. It contains near the stable ceiling a hinged door, opened and shut by a cord, and near the top of the building a damper to close in case of high winds. The damper is shown closed, as for a night of high winds. To open it pull the cord and wind it about the cleat shown. The damper is made of a board just the size of the inside of the ventilator. It is kept from falling down the ventilator by resting upon a cleat at one side and the damper rod at the other. It is not balanced, and its own weight causes it to fall across and close the shaft when the cord is loosened. The feed-door shown open must be tight when closed after throwing in hay. There should be several of these doors in the ventilator at different heights.

For controlling odors in the stable nothing equals fine road dust. Its absorptive quality is surprising. Never use lime nor ashes. They only set the ammonia free as an annoying and destroying gas to act upon the eyes of the horse, spoil the carriage varnish, and rot the harness.

The necessity for a harness closet, and an illustration of one, has already been given on page 56. Another great convenience about the stable is the wash-pave, where the carriage may be washed without getting it splashed with mud while doing it, or at the same time get your feet muddy. It should be somewhat larger on all sides than the carriage, and should be depressed towards the centre, with a gutter to run the water off. It may be made of flat flagging stones, bricks or concrete. Have it in a sheltered sunny place if possible, and the carriage will get washed on many winter days when otherwise it would not be done.

There is another chief stable necessity—pure water. Be sure it is pure. Impure water dulls the lustre of coat and eye, and numbs the action and other faculties, gradually poisoning the system and lessening the value of the horse, or destroying him if its use be continued. A stable or yard draining into or soaking through the soil to a barn well makes water impure, dangerous. If the purity be questioned, send a sample quart to the chemist of your State experiment station to be analyzed.

A home-made device for locking rolling stable doors which requires no key, and yet which is securely fastened, is shown in Figure 1.   Have a string go through the wall to raise the

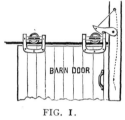

FIG. 1.

catch on the inside.

A very simple and cheap home-made latch for the barn door is shown in Figure 2. A, B and C are sticks of hard wood two inches square.   In A and B are cut notches at D and E an inch deep for the bolt C to slide in.   The bolt is also cut down, as shown in the drawing, sufficiently to allow it to work freely even in damp weather.   Screw the pieces A and B to the inside of the door.   Bevel the end of the bolt C at H

at such an angle that when the door shuts, and the bolt strikes the jamb J the bolt will be pushed back and fall into the slot in the jamb by its own weight.   Put a strong pin in the hole of the bolt at K, and make a slot in the door for this pin to work in.   Keep the bearings well greased.

FIG. 2.

Perhaps a better bolt, but one a little harder to make, is shown in Figure 3.   In it A is a spring made of hickory or

FIG. 3.

oak and set into the end of the bolt B.   At C is a flat strip of wood, which goes through the bolt and through a slot in the door to open it from the other side.   The bolt is beveled at the end so that it will slide back, and the spring will throw it into place every time, no matter how hard the door may be slammed.   A pin at D will prevent the bolt going too far.   If your barn doors are cut through at the middle, as they should be, the hickory spring A could

be continued up above the top of the lower door and the pin
c dispensed with. This is a good arrangement where children are around. While they can push back the pin and open
the door, they are not able to reach to the top of the door
and push back the spring.

Have a place for everything, and, what is of more importance, see that everything is put in its place. Neat and
convenient hooks for the stable tools and
brushes will save time and temper, aside
from keeping everything orderly about
the stable. The little illustration speaks
for itself.

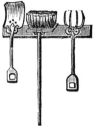

Herewith are given the ground plans
and elevations of three different stables,
in which those contemplating building or
altering may find some helpful hints even
if the plan is not adopted in full. The stables may be constructed of whatever material the builder may desire, and as
the localities in which this book will be read are so widely
separated, and the price of materials consequently so variable,
it is impossible to give any accurate estimate of their cost.
For the reason that we have not room to give the plans of
large general-purpose barns, the plans given are those of
stables alone; but the arrangement or suggestions in the
drawings may well be followed in planning quarters for
horses in large barns.

There are many people living on small lots and in villages
who need stable room for only one horse and perhaps a cow.
The stable here shown is an excellent one. The framework
of the whole is 18 by 25 feet. The carriage room is 9 by 18.
A foot or two more in its width would not be amiss and
would then give space for the carriage, sleigh, lawn-mower,
etc., besides room for unhitching in stormy weather and for

cleaning harness. By the way, the harness should be hung up on pins in this room, away from the ammonia generated in

ELEVATION SHOWING SMALL VILLAGE STABLE.

the stable. The horse, as will be seen in the plan, can be taken directly into the stable without going out-of-doors.

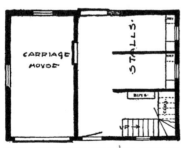

PLAN OF SMALL VILLAGE STABLE.

Straw and hay are stored in the lofts above, reached by the flight of stairs, as shown. The arrangement of the loft may be according to the wishes and needs of the builder.

The plan of the stalls without an entry in front, as shown, while very common and economical of space, is not a good one if it can be avoided, as all the feed has to be carried in alongside of the animal. When a cow is kept in a stall of this kind there is always danger of her throwing her horns around and injuring her attendant.

Some may prefer a hinged door to the carriage room, but the rolling one has the advantage of never blowing about in a high wind and is easily opened and shut under all circumstances, including a big snowdrift right up against it. The plan has been drawn to the scale of sixteen feet to the inch.

The second plan and elevation show a stable larger than the preceding, and is one designed by a member of the *Farm*

A THREE-HORSE STABLE.

Journal staff. It has been in use for several years, and has proven to be very satisfactory and convenient. There is stabling for three horses, and by doing away with the harness-closet four may be accommodated. The covered driveway in front will be found almost indispensable—for hitching and unhitching, for washing the carriage on the washpave, (shown in the plan,) for cleaning the horses, etc.

The harness-closet should have been shown with a window in it, and should be made as tight as possible of tongued and grooved boards. The stairway leads up from the entry to the second floor, which contains a good-sized room for the man to sleep in, a storage room for grain, a mow for hay over the carriage room, and one for straw over the stalls. The hay is thrown down the chute into the entry, and the straw down the chute back of the stalls. The location of the chutes is shown by dotted lines. The manure pit is conveniently placed just alongside of the back door, where drains in the cemented floor of the stalls lead the liquid manure. Either end of the shed may be boarded up if

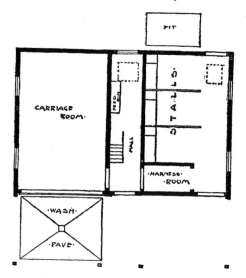

necessary to make it more protected from storms. This plan has also been drawn to the scale of sixteen feet to the inch.

The third stable shown is much more pretentious, having accommodations for seven horses and half-a-dozen carriages. There is a good-sized harness-room, a large areaway for inside ungearing, two box stalls, a good-sized feeding entry, watering trough, a ventilating shaft, and other conveniencies. Under the stairs leading to the second floor there is a closet. The second floor furnishes abundance of room for the man, storage for hay, grain and straw, and a carpenter's room for working in on rainy days could be easily located. The box stalls open on the outside as well as into the stable.

STABLE FOR SEVEN HORSES.

In this plan the space devoted to carriages could no doubt be advantageously reduced, as the room shown is about 26 by 32 feet.

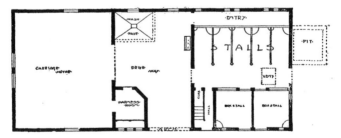

In conclusion, it might be said that each builder should make the measurements which are best suited to his wants. These plans are merely presented as suggestions and aids in the arrangement and location of the different essential parts of the stable.

INDEX.